Written by Alexander Finbow, illustrated by Nyco Rudolph
Logo, cover design, typesetting and production by Ryan Ferrier

For Karen, Janelle, Leia & Phoebe

When Big Bears Invade, conceived and written by Alexander Finbow. First published in Canada 2017 by Renegade Arts Canmore Ltd trading as Renegade Arts Entertainment Ltd.

ISBN 9781987825497

Office of Publication 25 Prospect Heights, Canmore, Alberta T1W 2S2

Renegade Arts Entertainment is
Alexander Finbow Doug Bradley Alan Grant John Finbow
Luisa Harkins Emily Pomeroy Sean Tonelli

Printed April 2017 in Canada by Friesens.

Check out more titles from Renegade Arts Entertainment in good book and comic stores and at our website:

RenegadeArtsEntertainment.com

* Poutine is pronounced poutin, who knew.
* Feel free to add 'DUUUUUDE!' after the rhyme on the Vancouver page.

'Children, children, gather round.
Stop the game, shush the sound.

I'll tell you a tale of greed.
Power sought, avarice decreed.

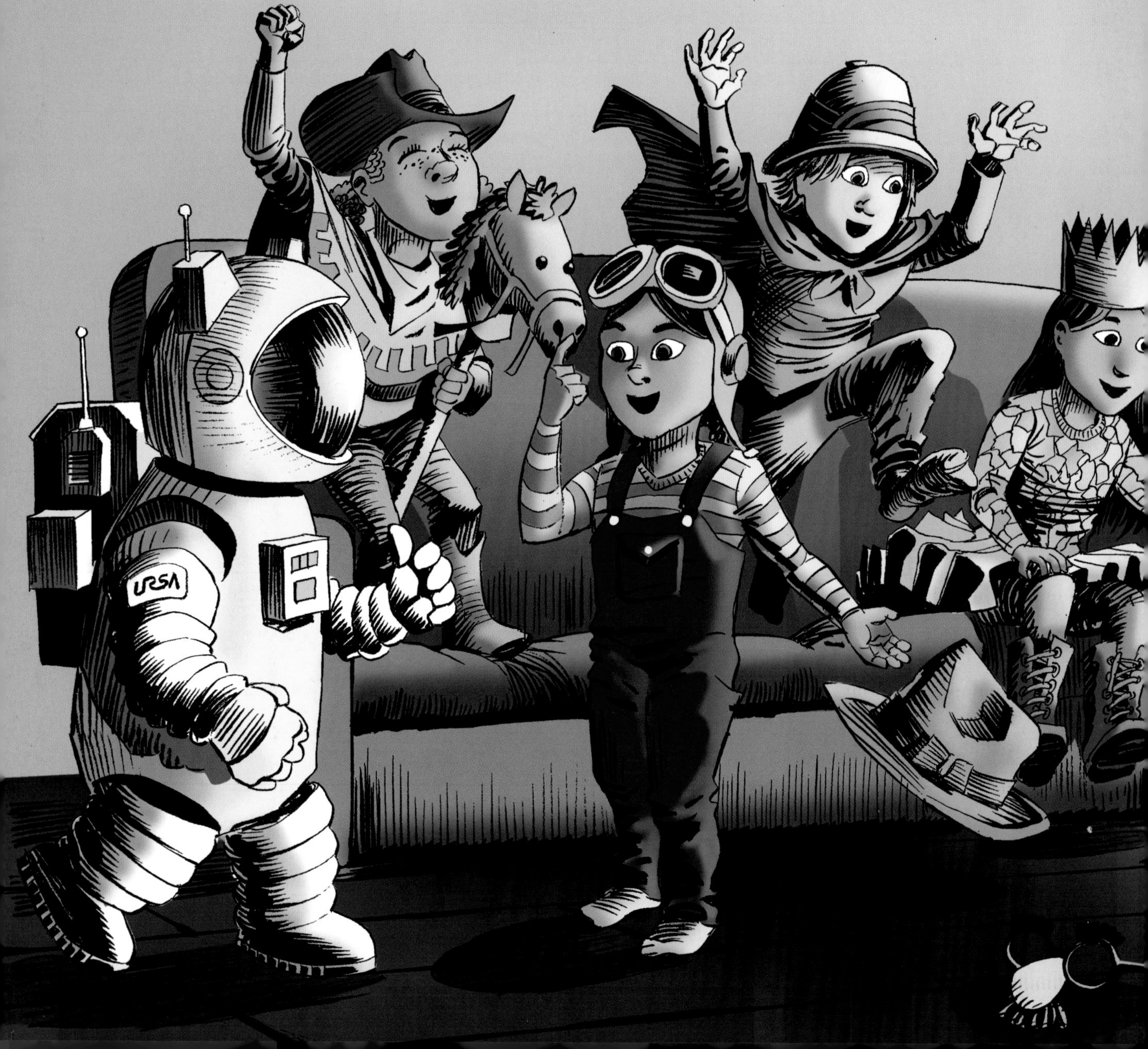
URSA

A time when Canadians were hasty,
At destroying our world like crazy.

A time when the benevolent bears,
Made sure humanity remembers, it cares.

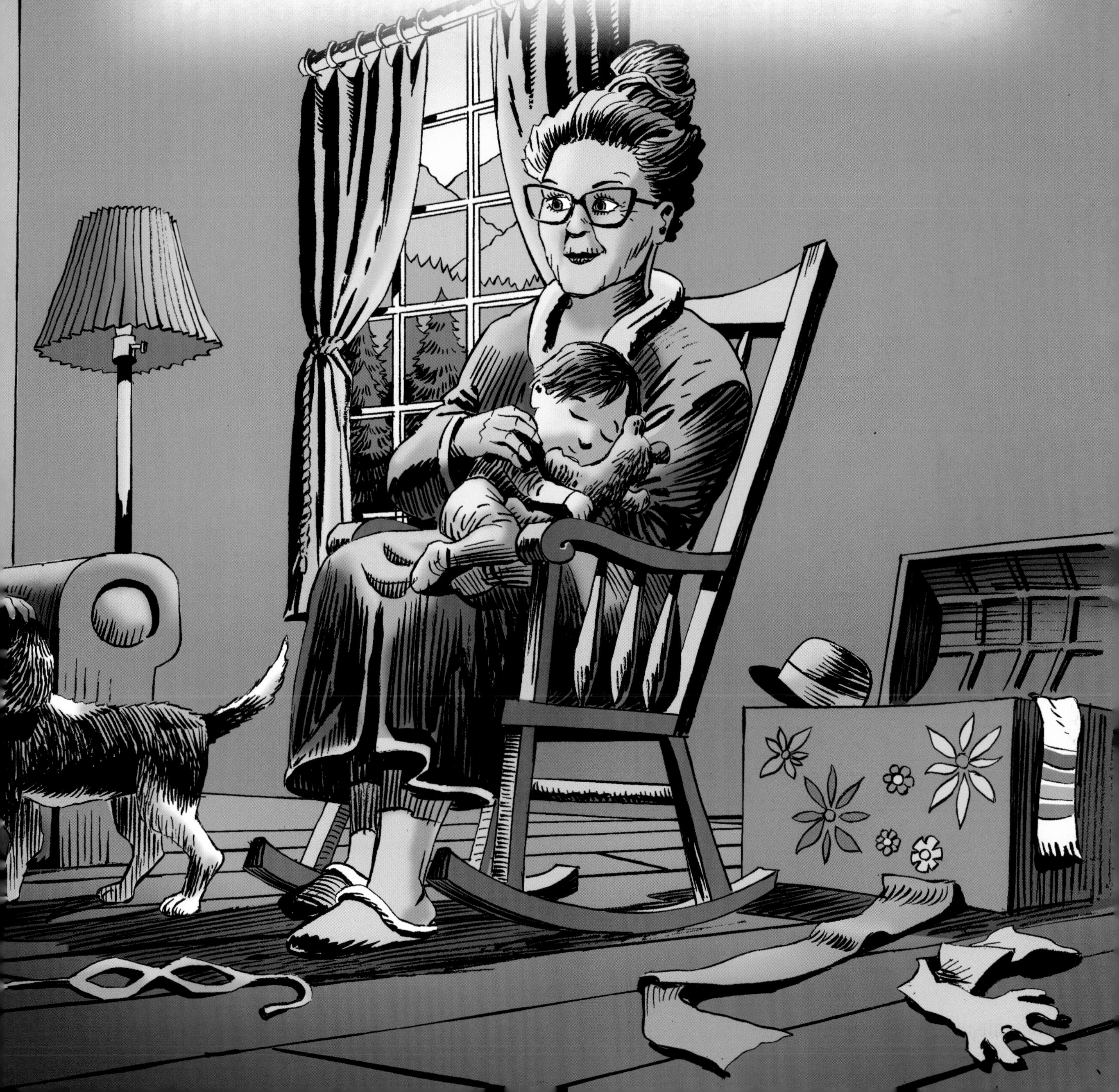

Do you know what first we saw?
A hole in the ground shaped like a paw.
We thought it a prank, a joke or a gag,
To birth a meme, get tongues to wag.

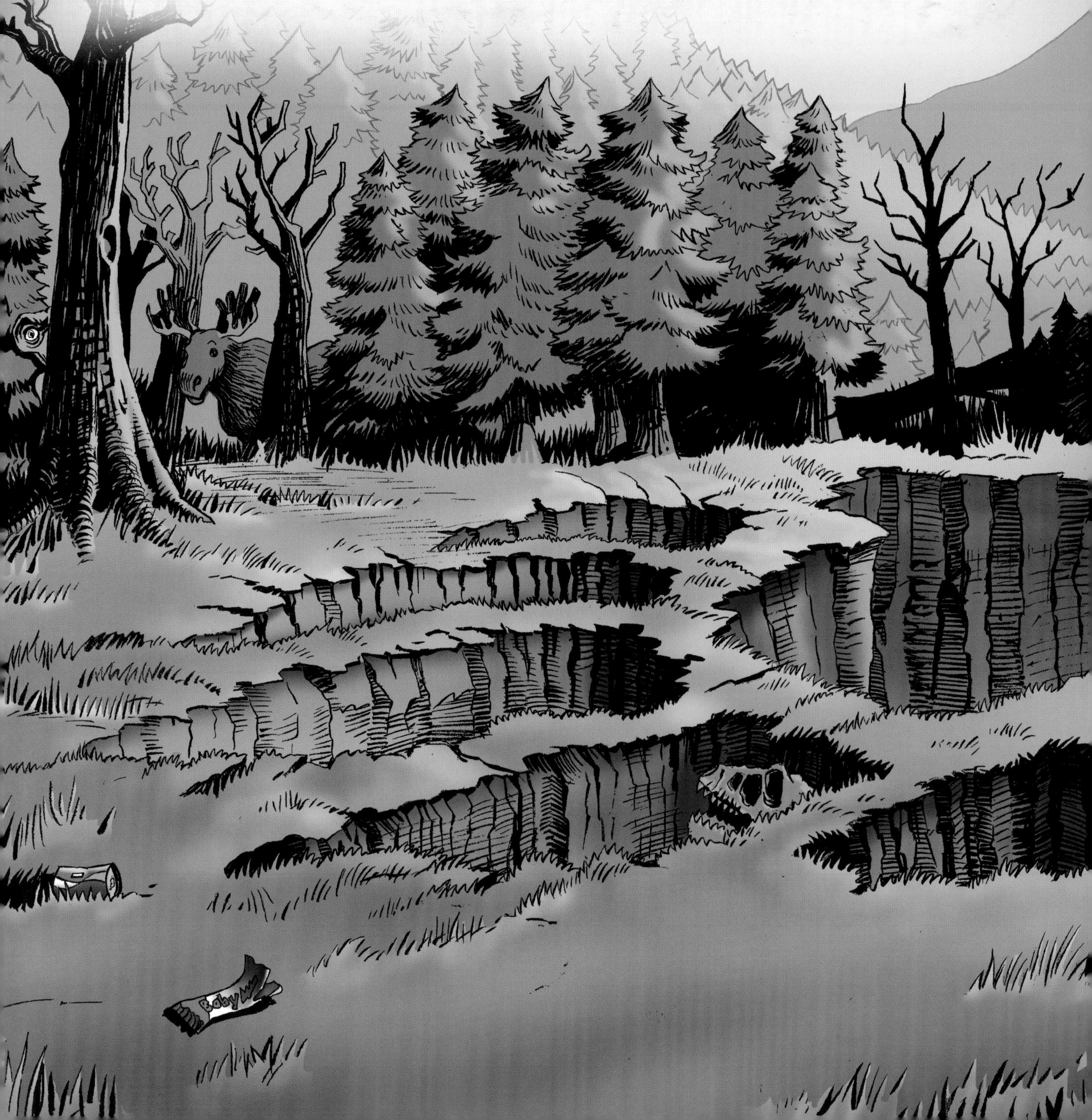

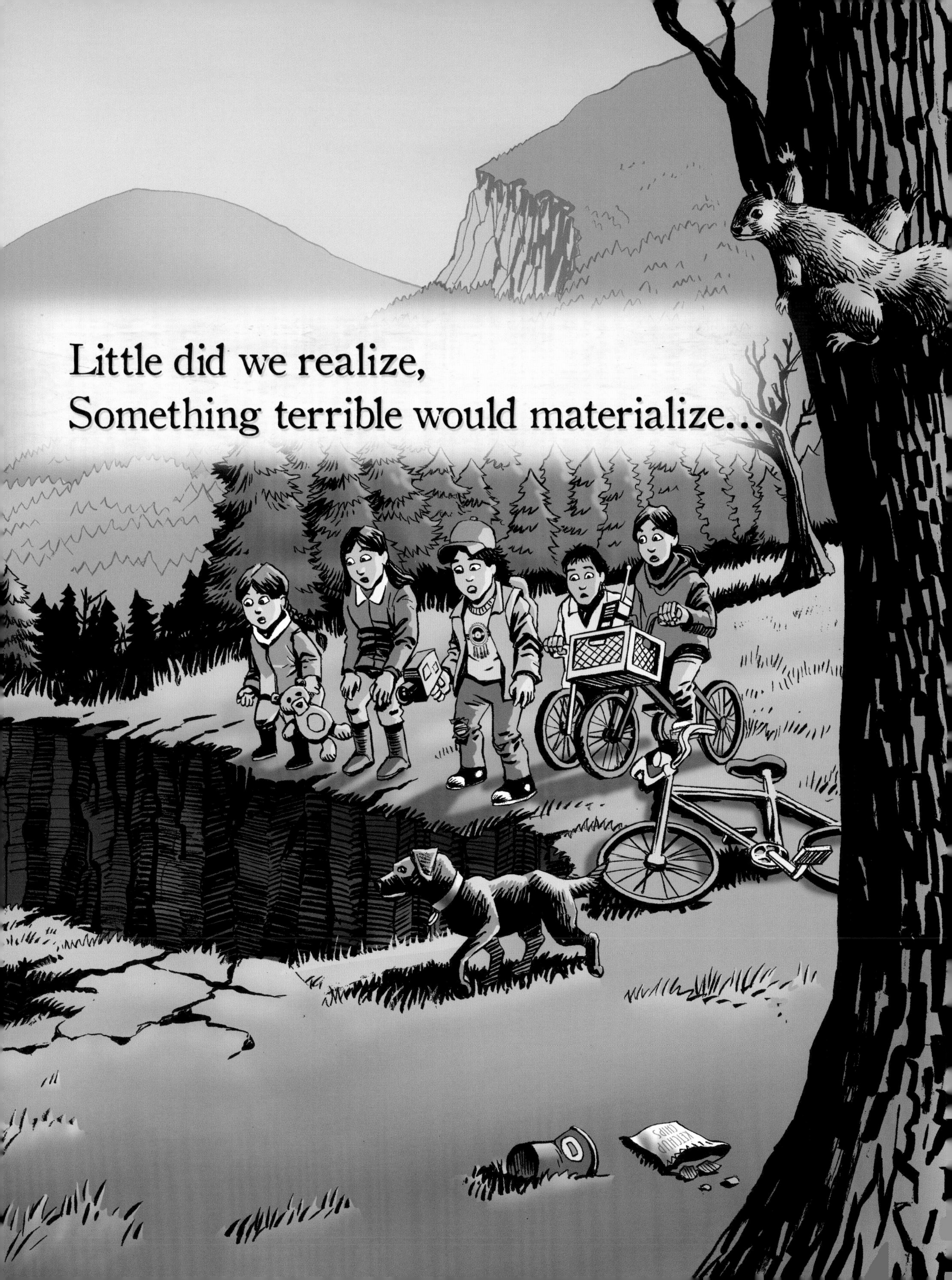
Little did we realize,
Something terrible would materialize...

Called together to form a whole,
Canada's bears had just one goal.

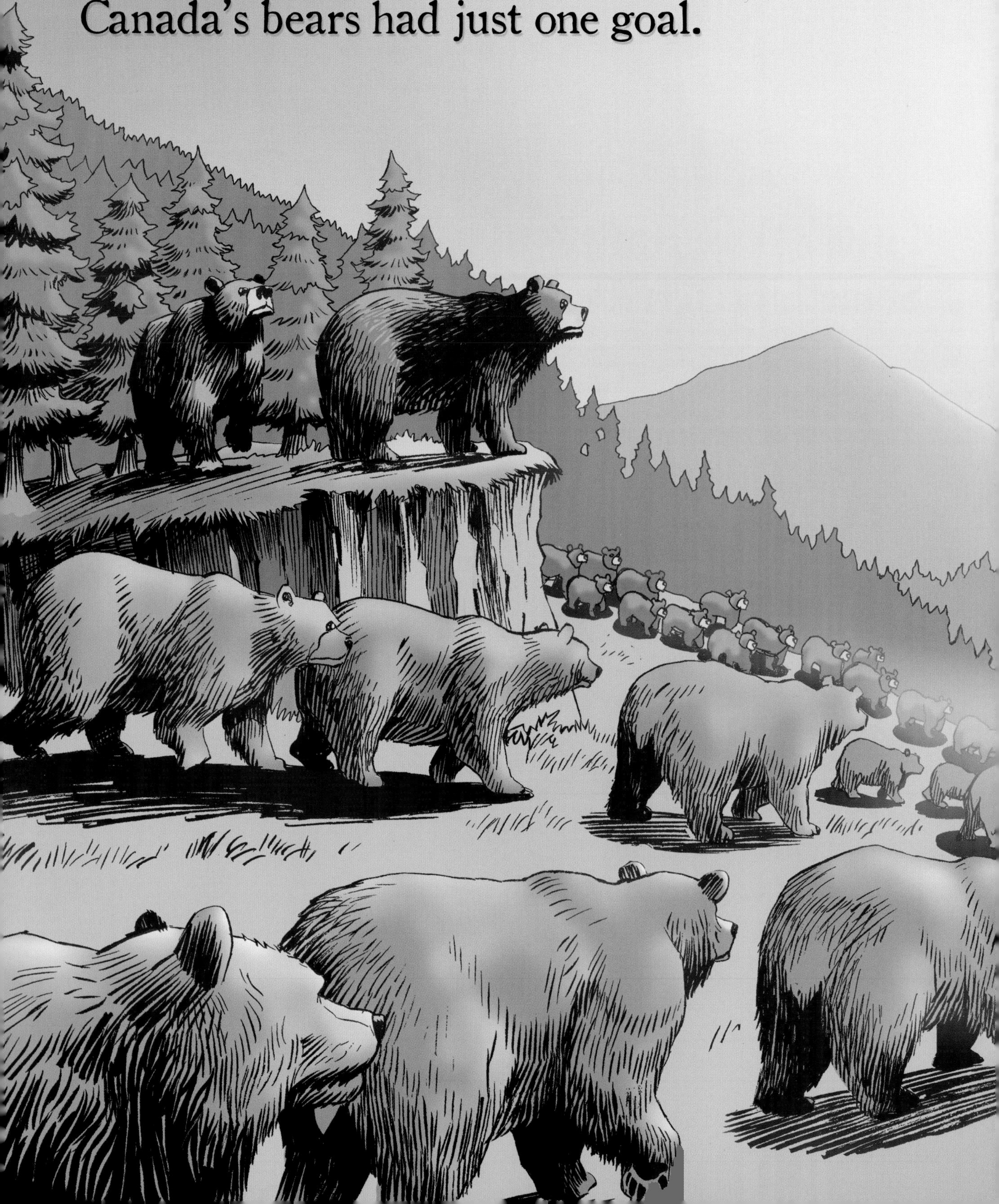

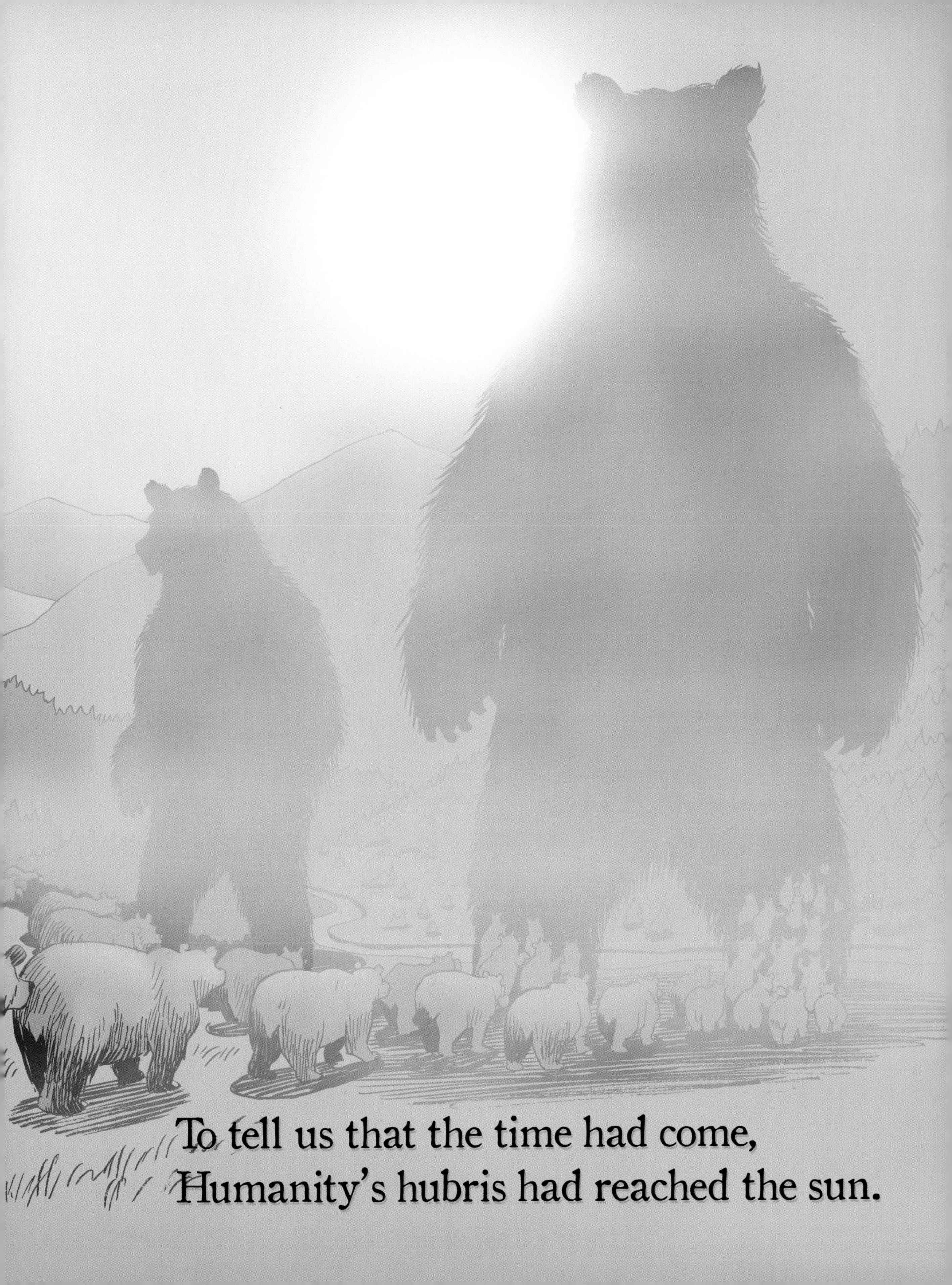

To tell us that the time had come,
Humanity's hubris had reached the sun.

Toronto was first in line,
A Giant Grizzly took her time.
To use the Tower as a broom,
And sweep the condos down, *BOOM*!

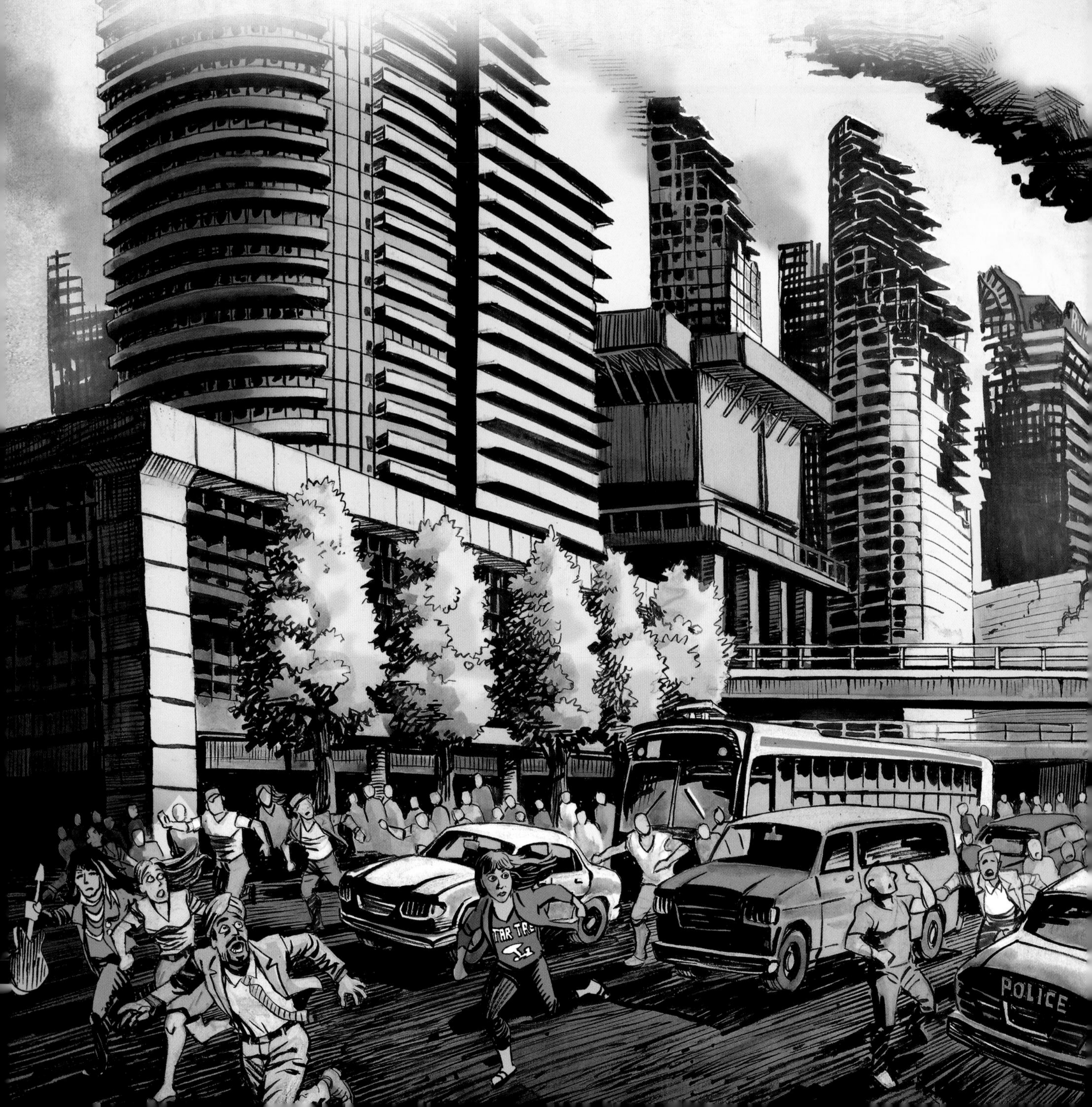
POLICE

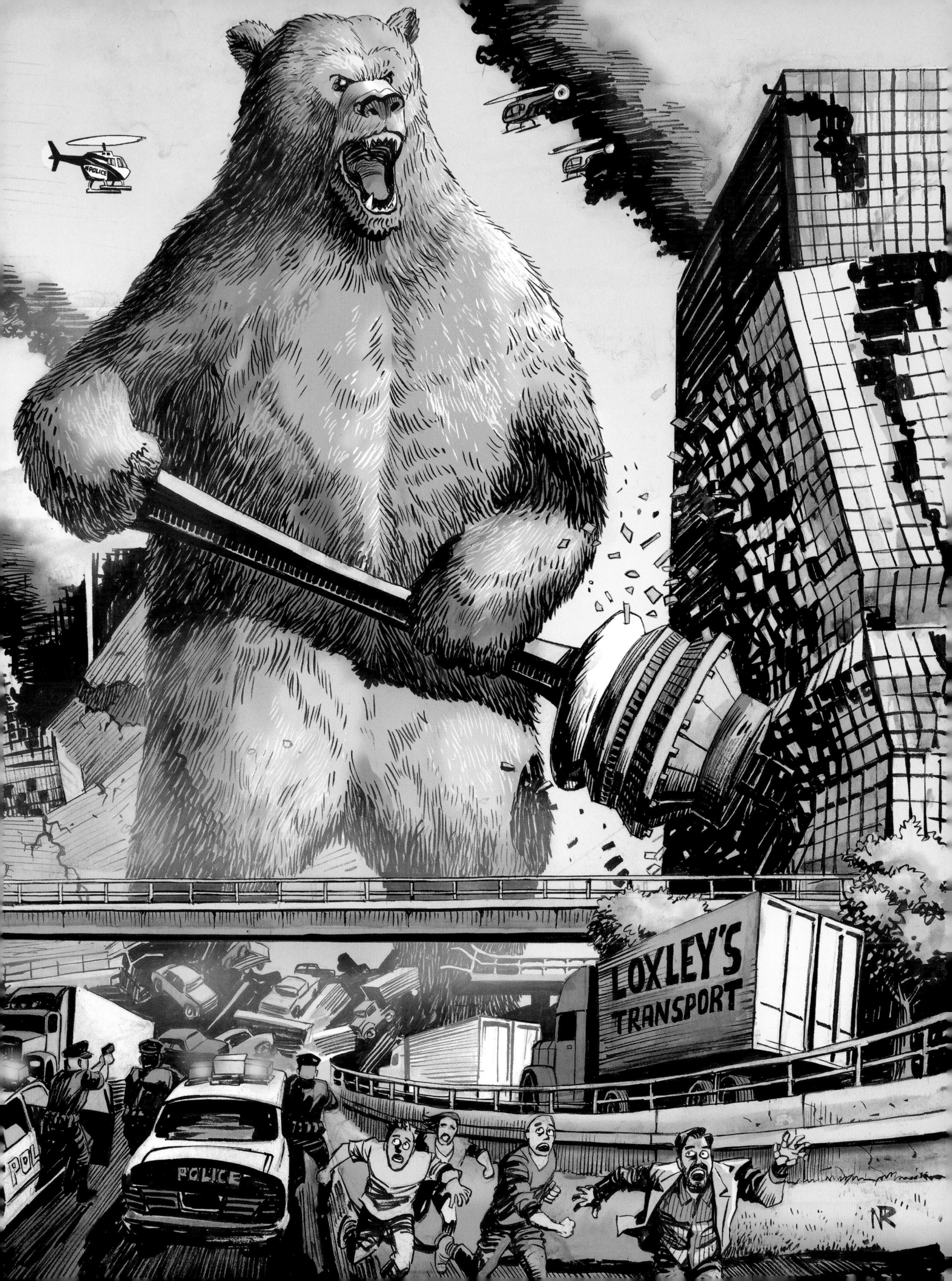
POLICE
LOXLEY'S
TRANSPORT
POLICE
POL

Oil Sands were on their list,
Did you *really* think they'd be missed?

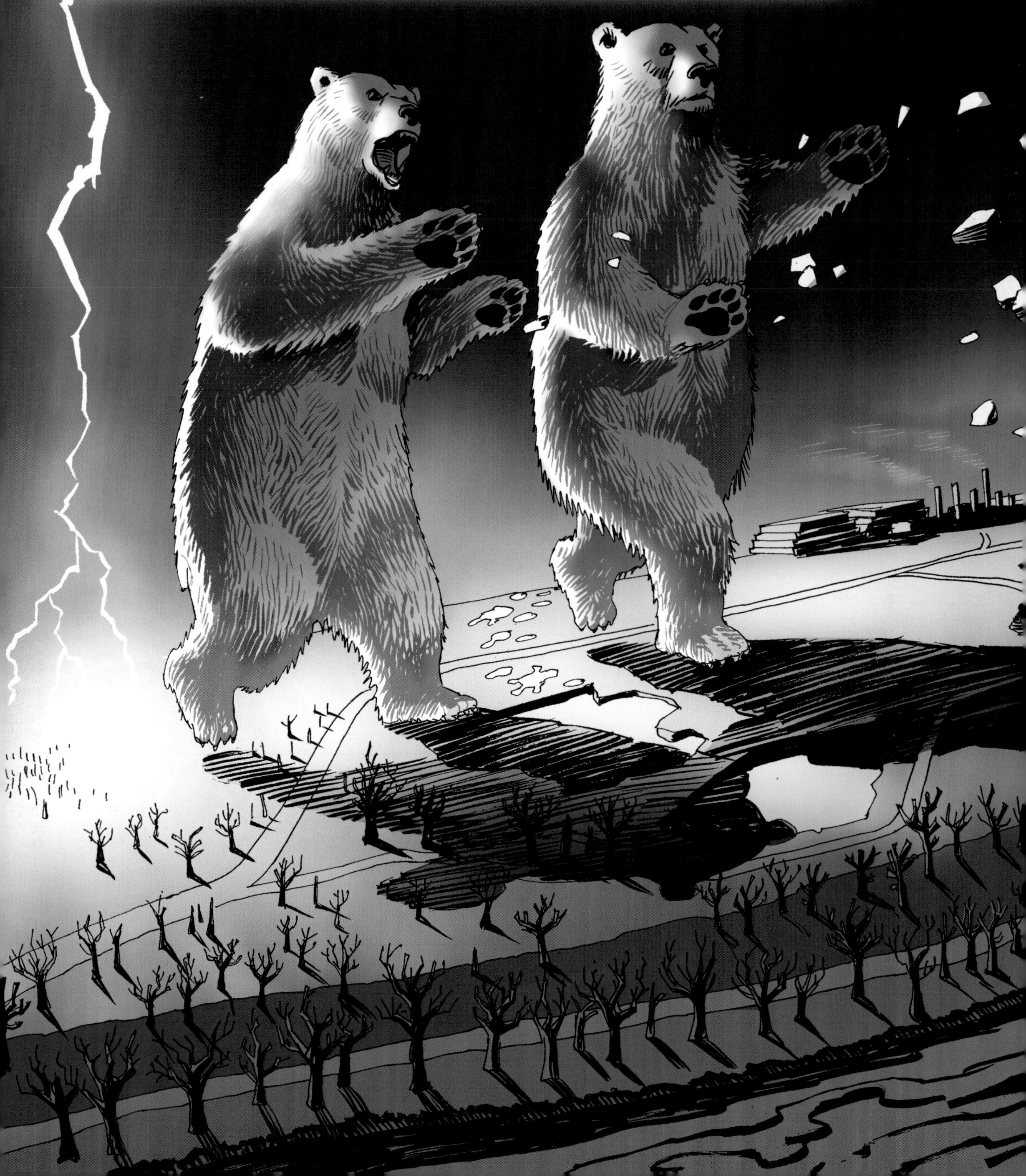

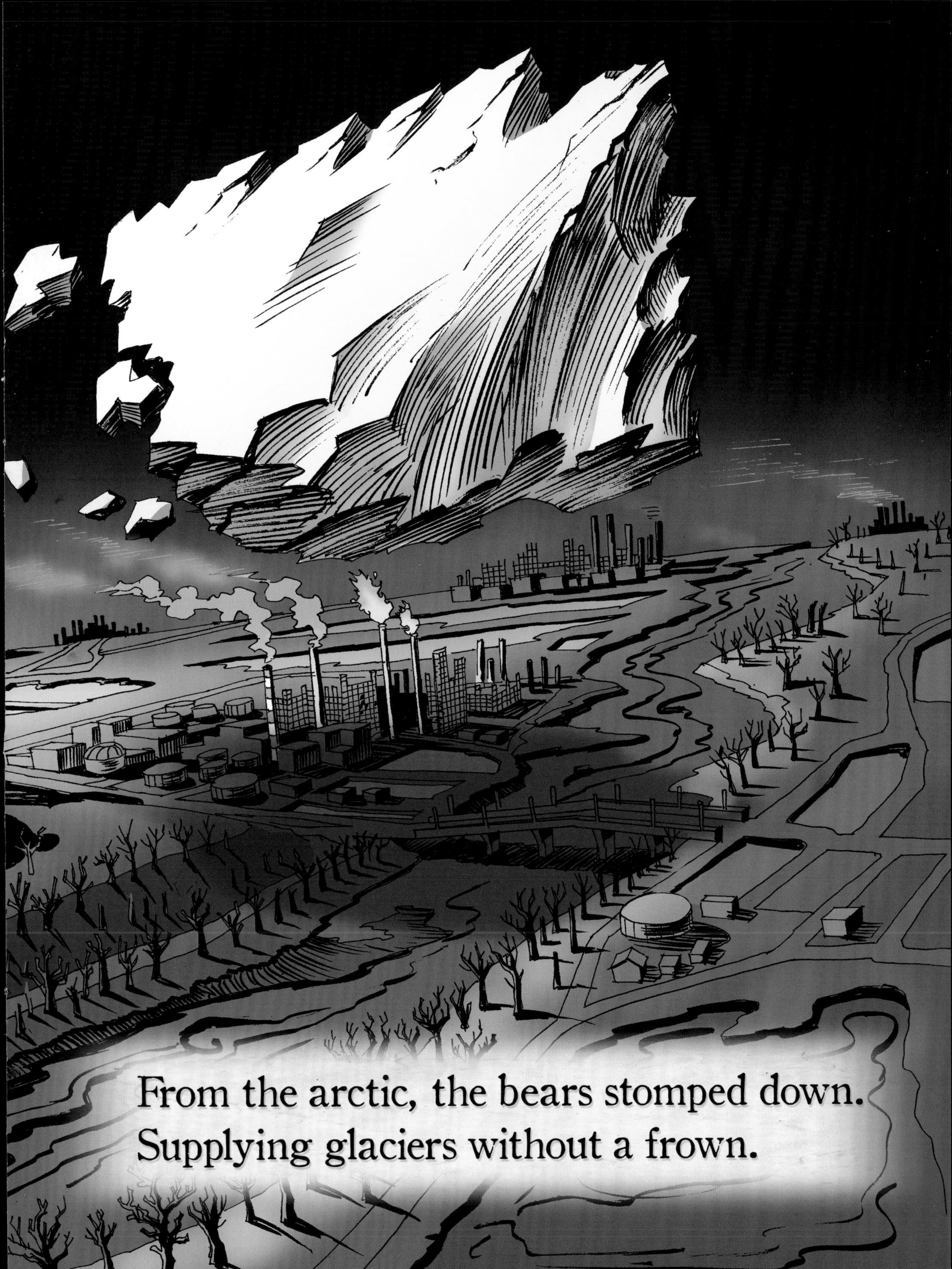
From the arctic, the bears stomped down.
Supplying glaciers without a frown.

From the west tsunami came,
Spirit Bears rode to fame.

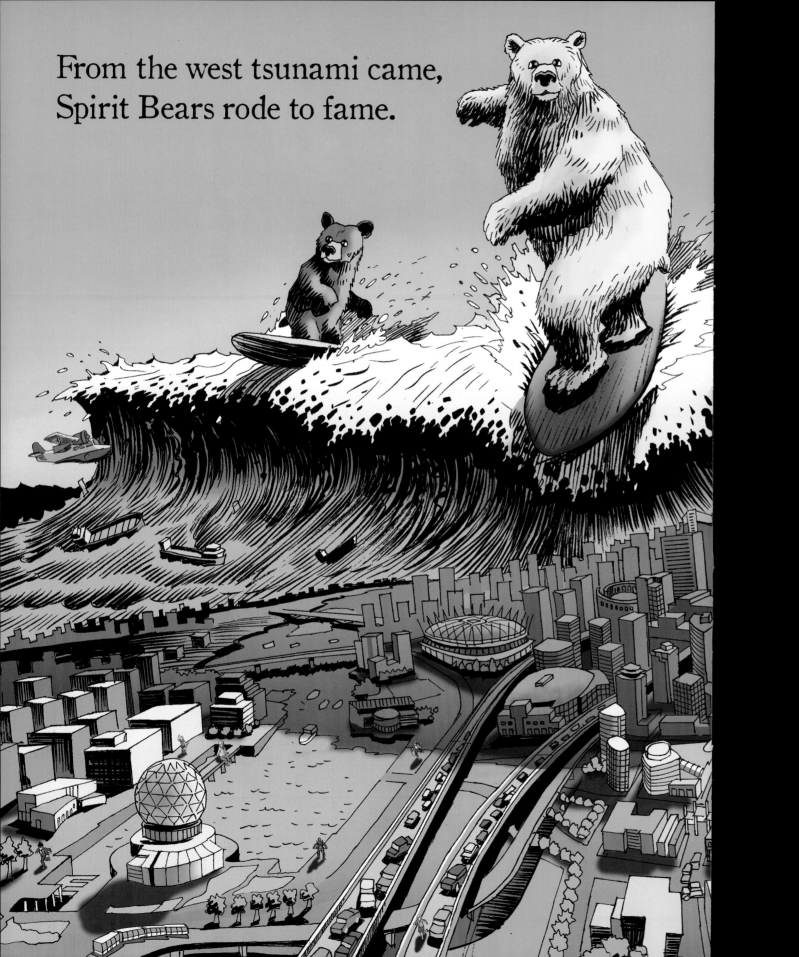

On a stick they ripped, completely stoked!
As Vancouver sank, totally soaked.

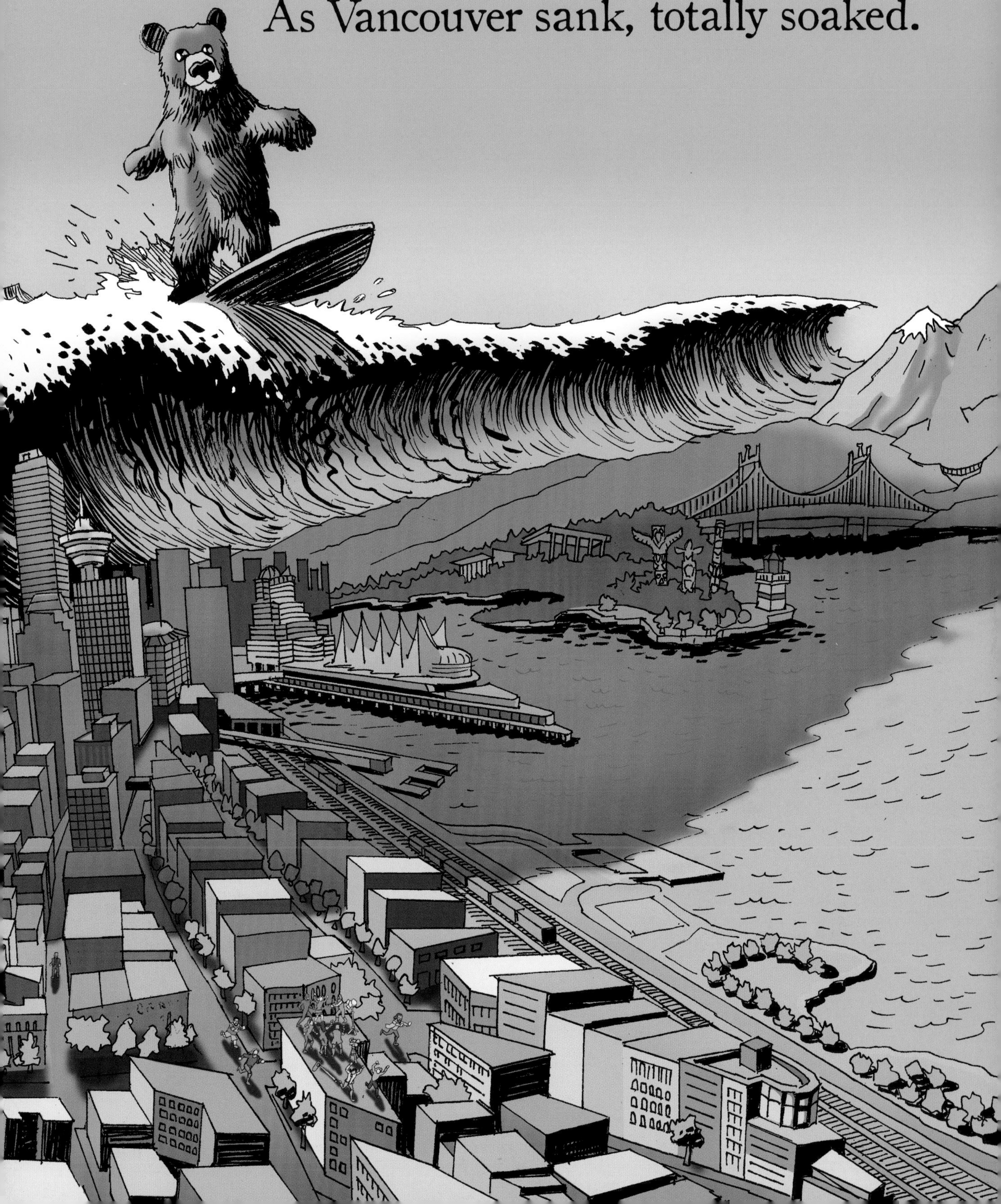

In Edmonton they arrived with haste,
As a mighty hockey game took place.

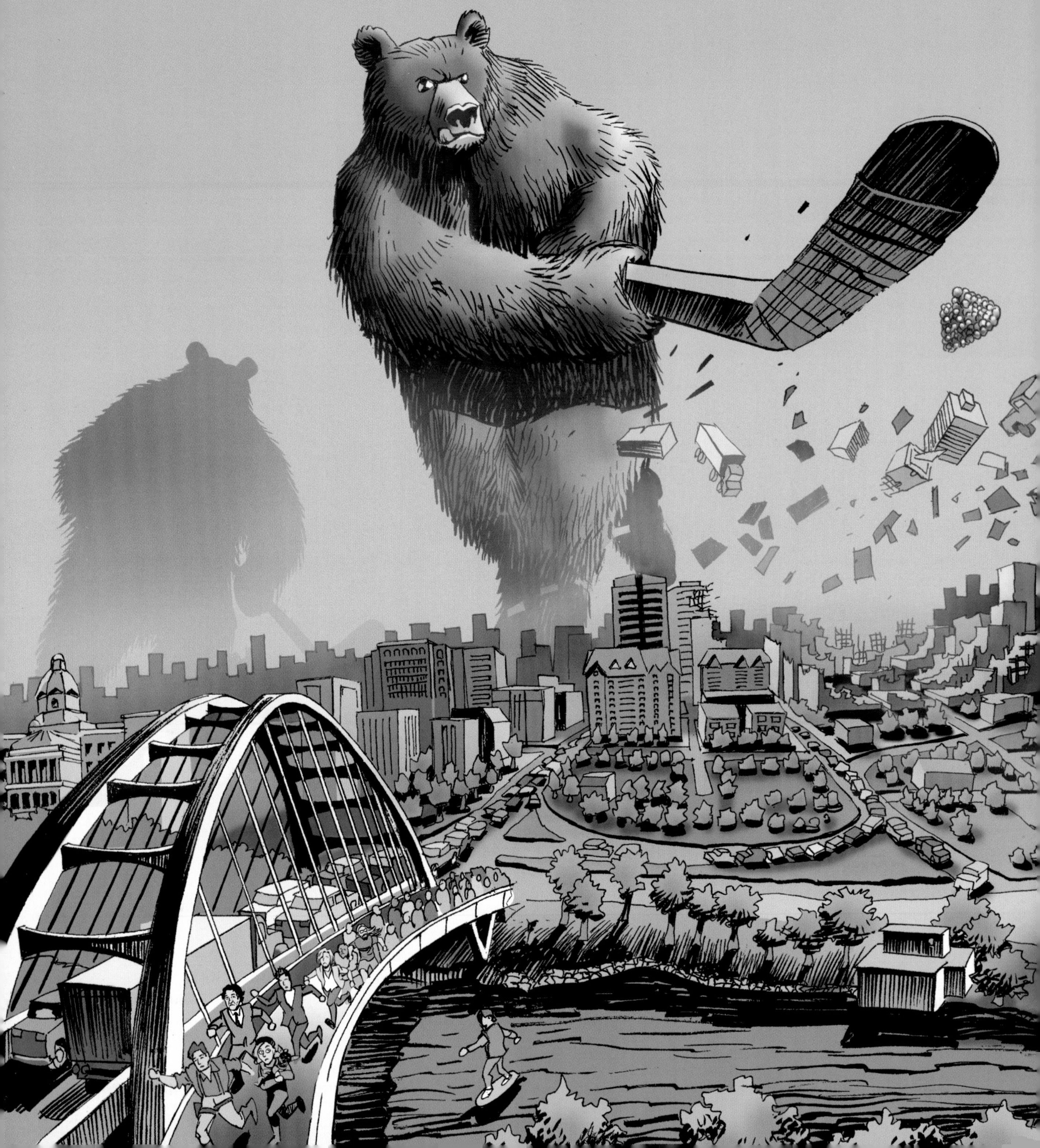

Their shiny arena became the puck,
Ploughed through the city, so out of luck.

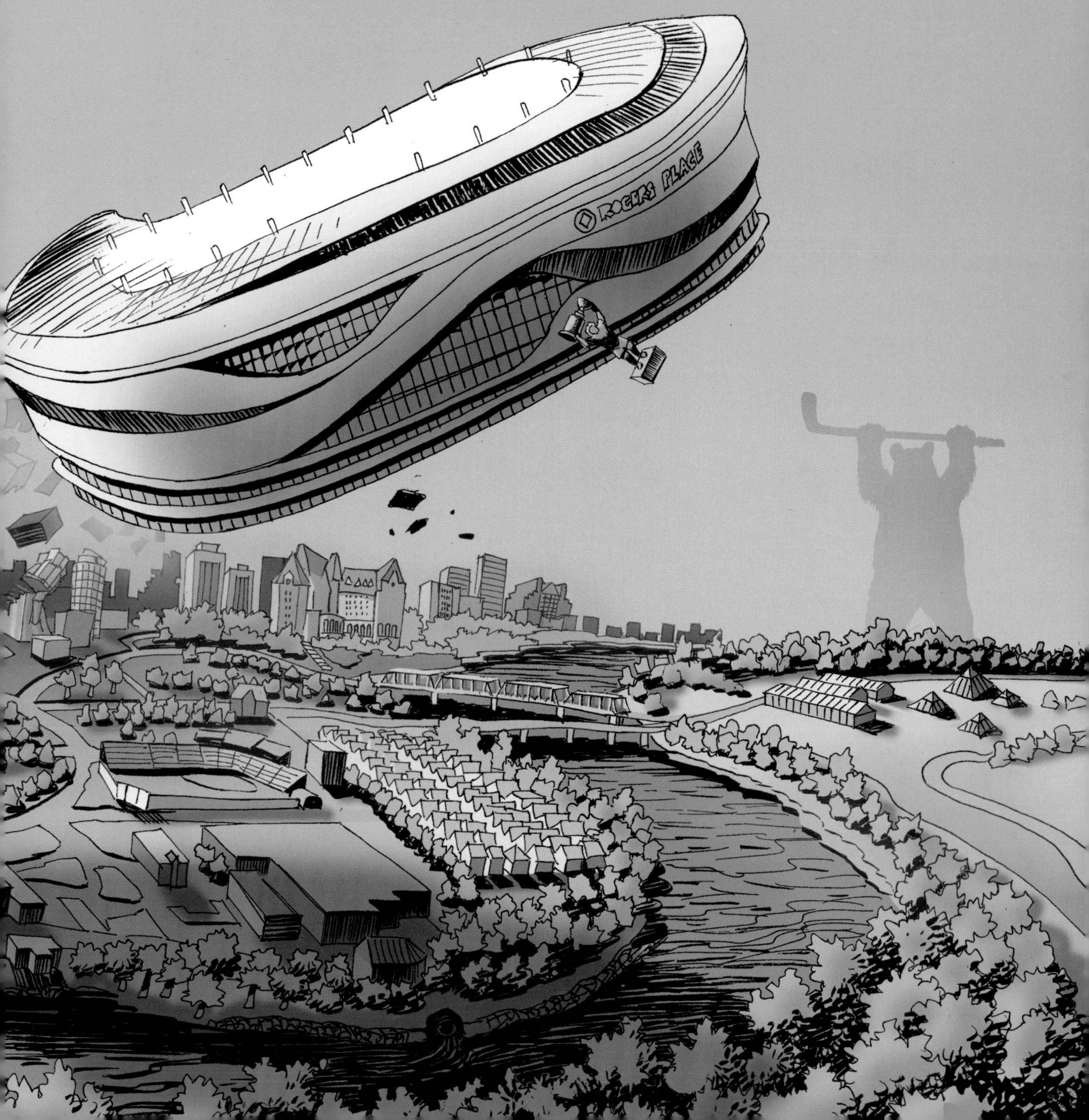
ROGERS PLACE

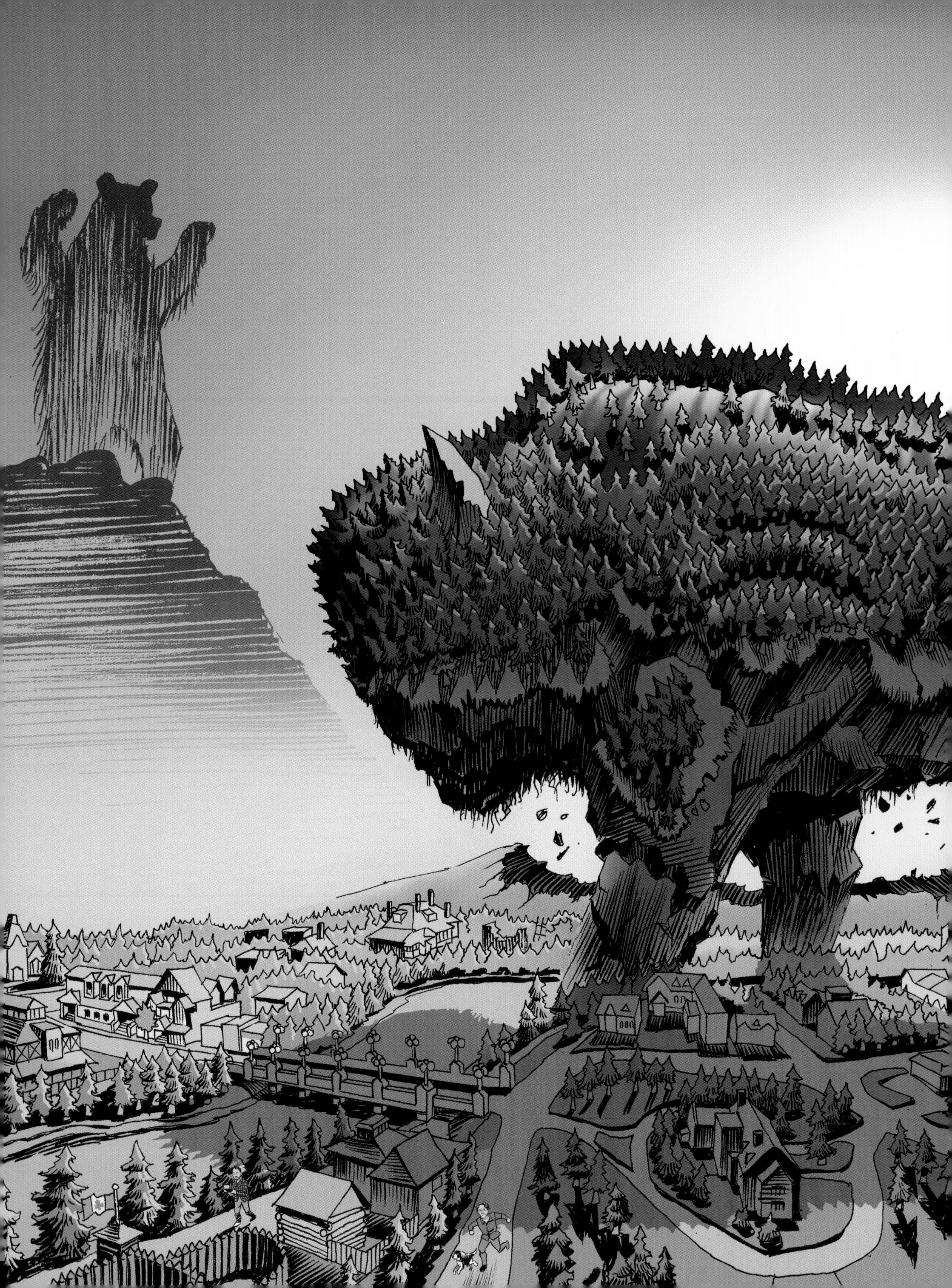

Sacred Buffalo Guardian called awake,
By a Banff bear shaman out to take.
All the tourists from their land.
It all kicked off just as planned.

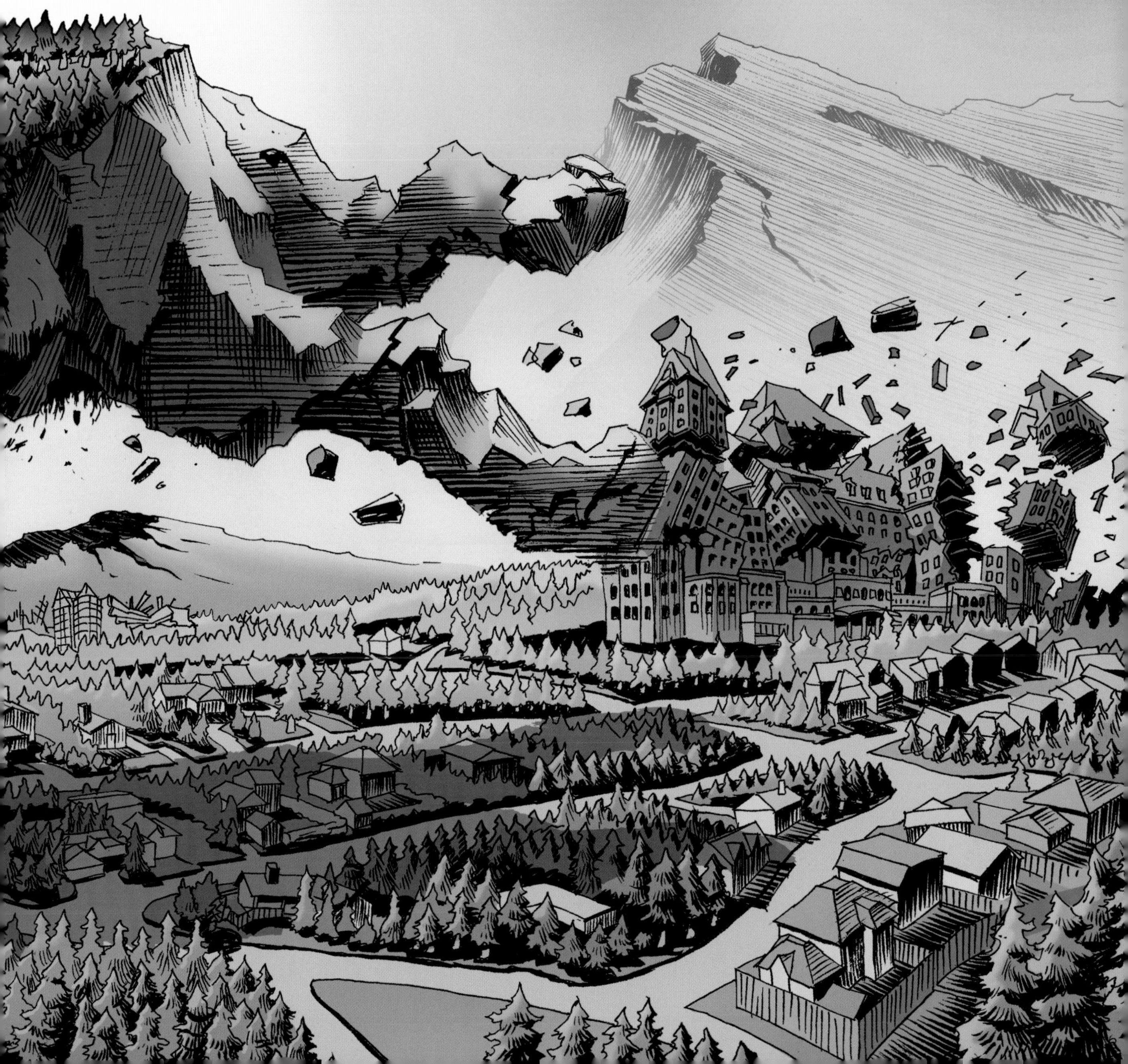

Winnipeg became the scene,
Of the greatest match there's ever been.

This frozen city is their sheet,
With popsicle people beneath their feet.

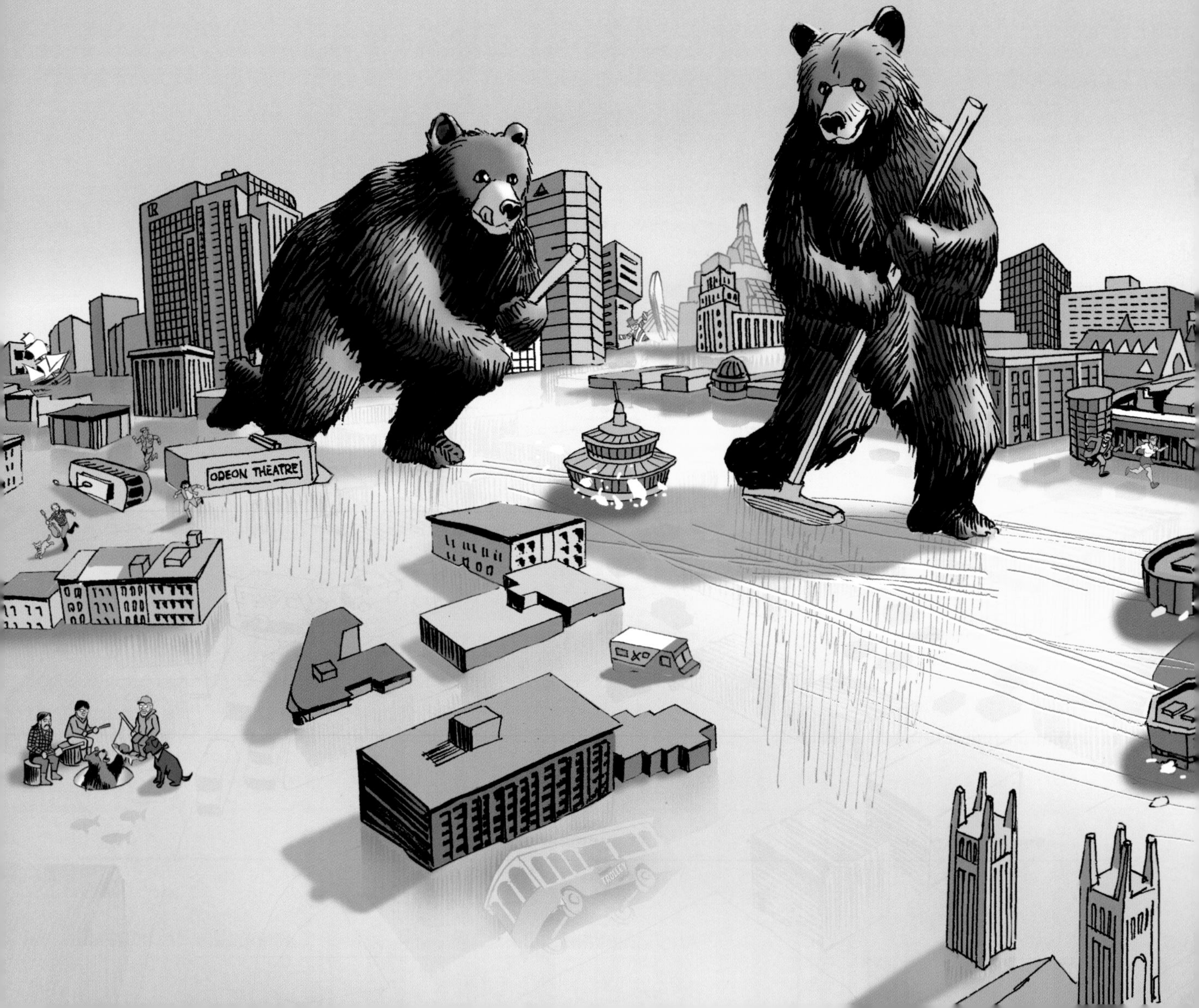
ODEON THEATRE

The polar bears think they've won,
This hammer shot may spoil their fun.

Black bears scream 'Hurry hard! Sweep hard!'
And slip their stone right past the guard.

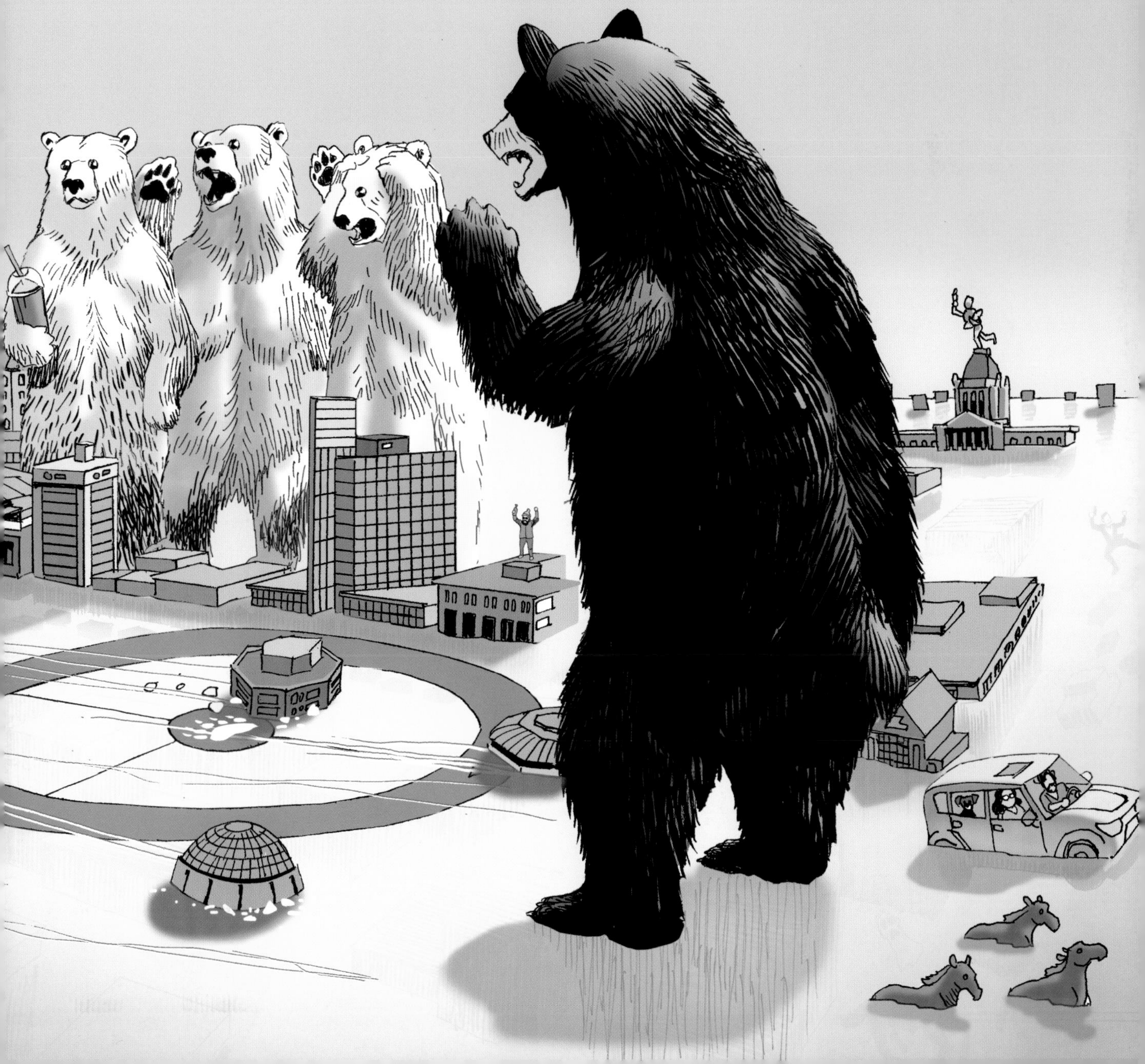

'But Gran!' They cried out all at once.
'This can't be true, we know it can't!

'Toronto was there, last week we thought.
And High Tea in Banff is so highly sought.'

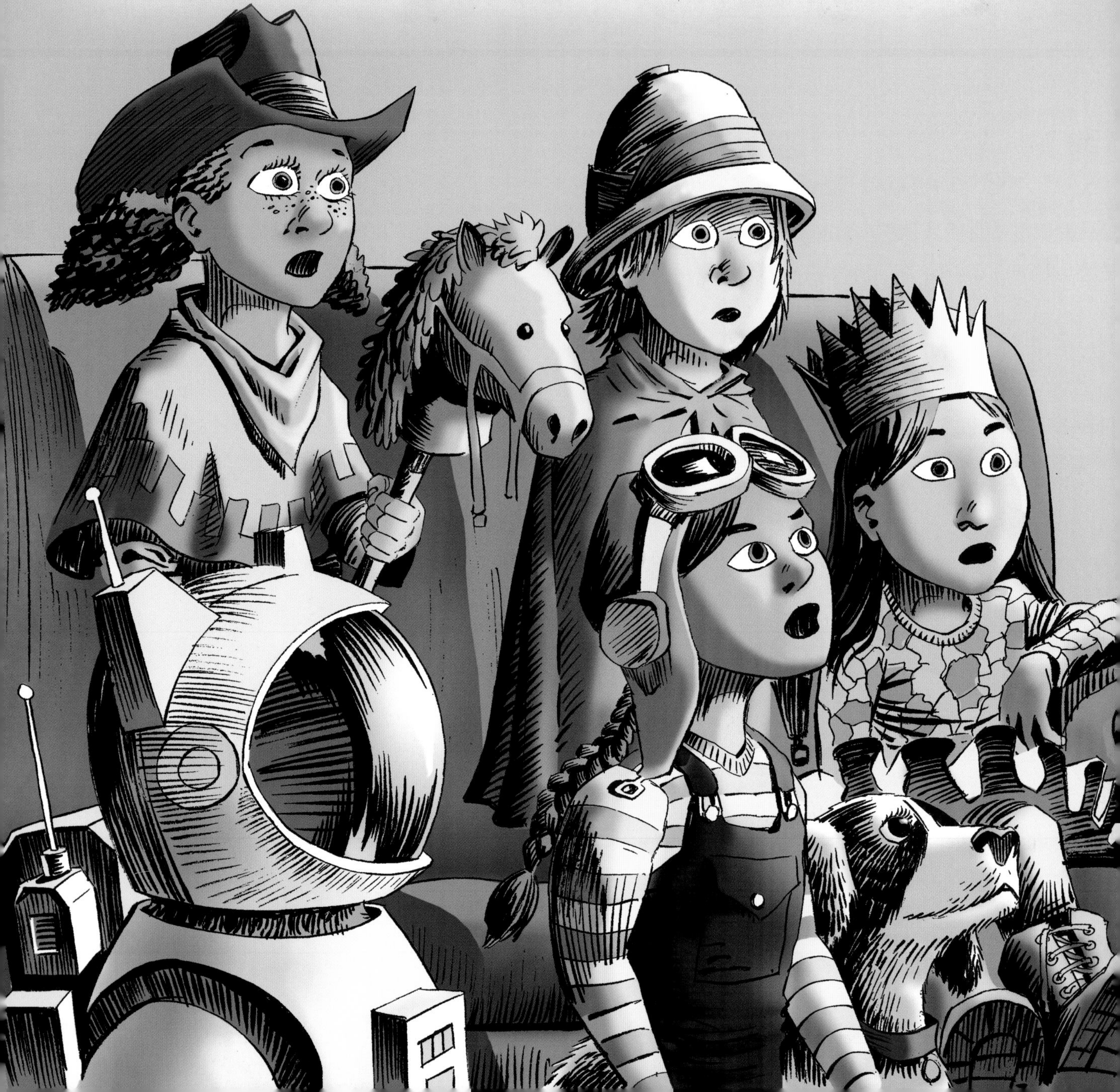

'But children are you sure?' She said.
'Trust your Grandmother, not what you've read.
The internet is full of lies,
Sit down, relax.
Hear how a city flies.'

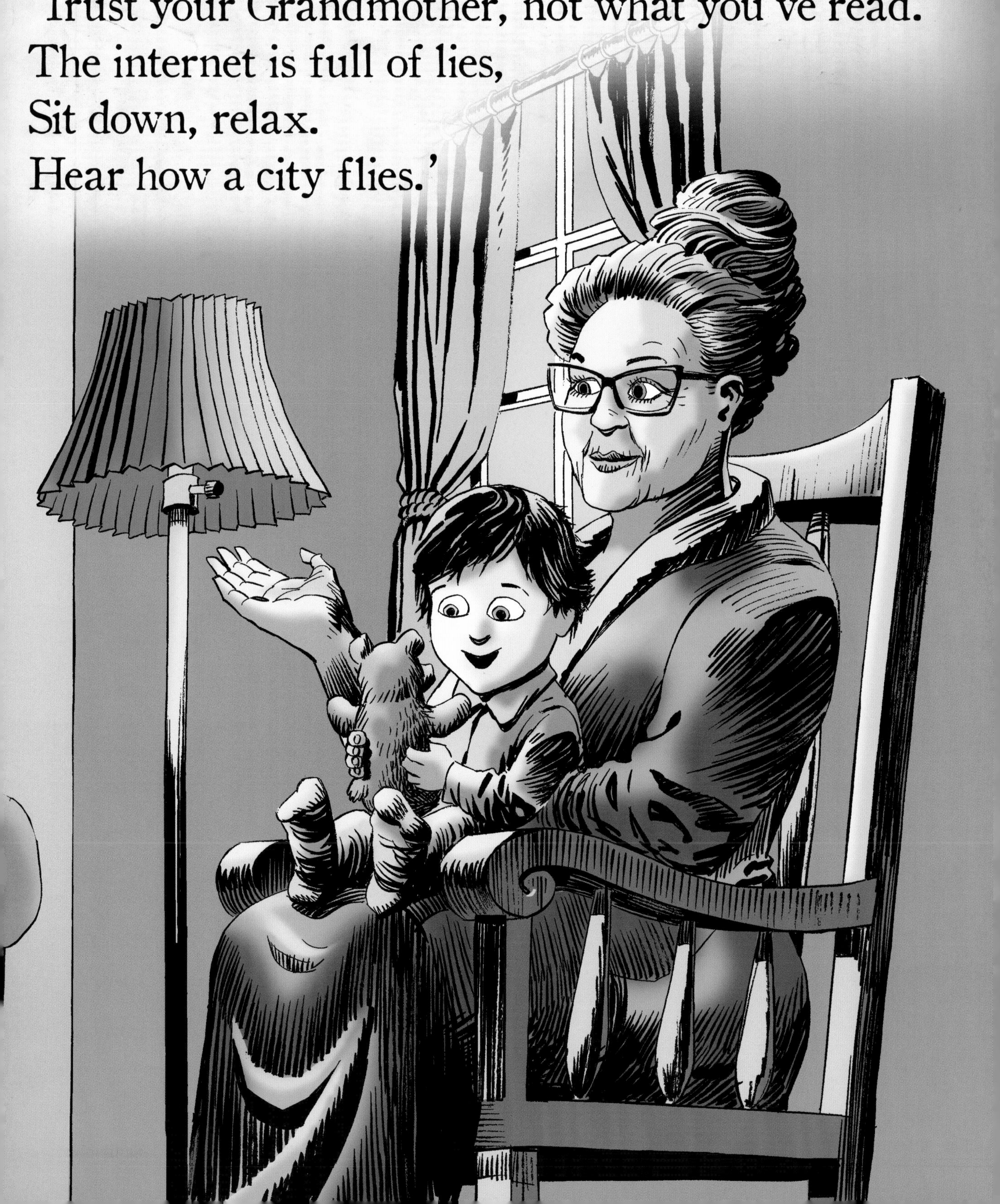

In Calgary, she came at dawn.
Ready to sleep, content to yawn.

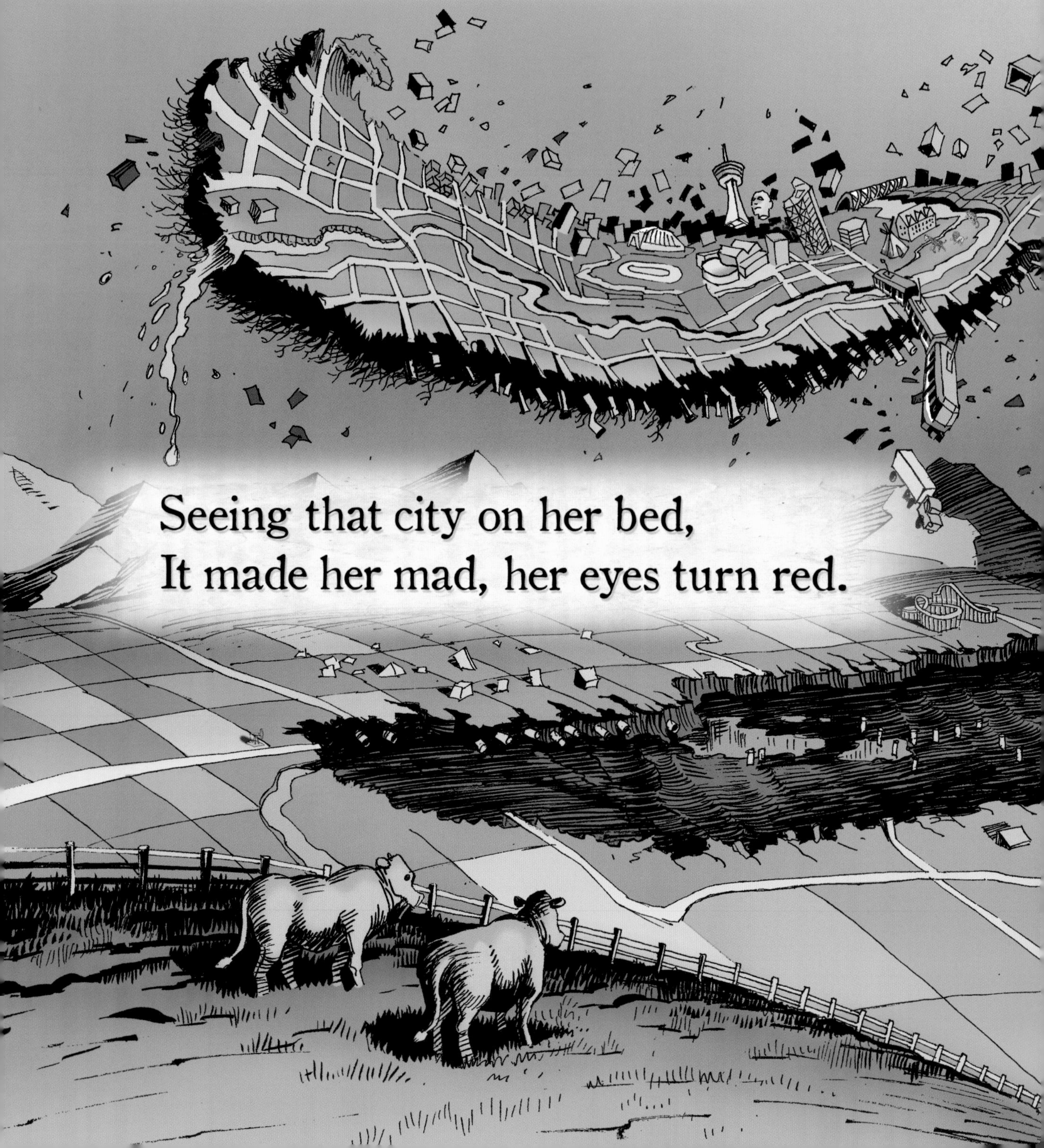

Seeing that city on her bed,
It made her mad, her eyes turn red.

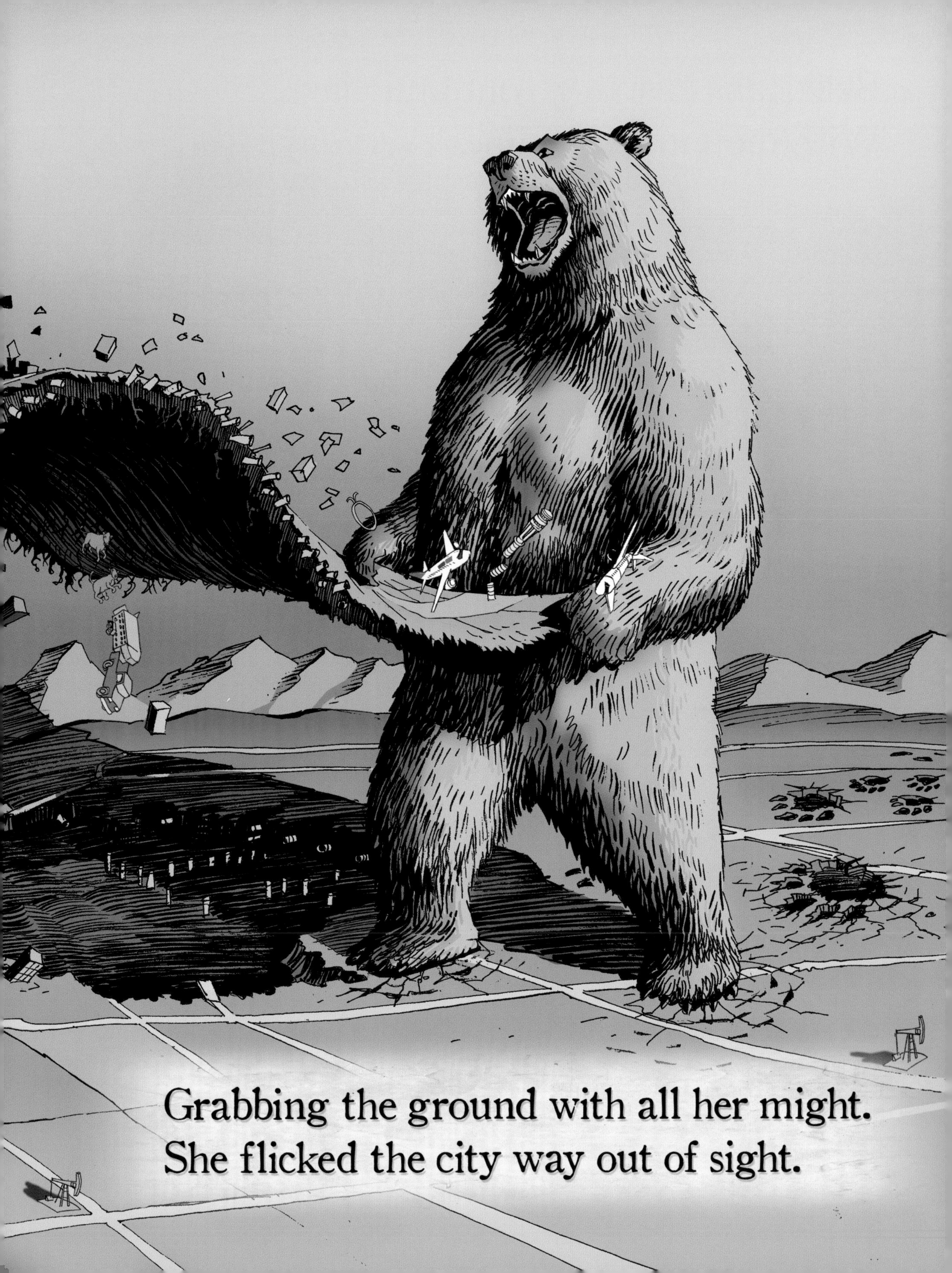

Grabbing the ground with all her might.
She flicked the city way out of sight.

Bear cubs love to go out and play,
With mountain pipelines everyday.

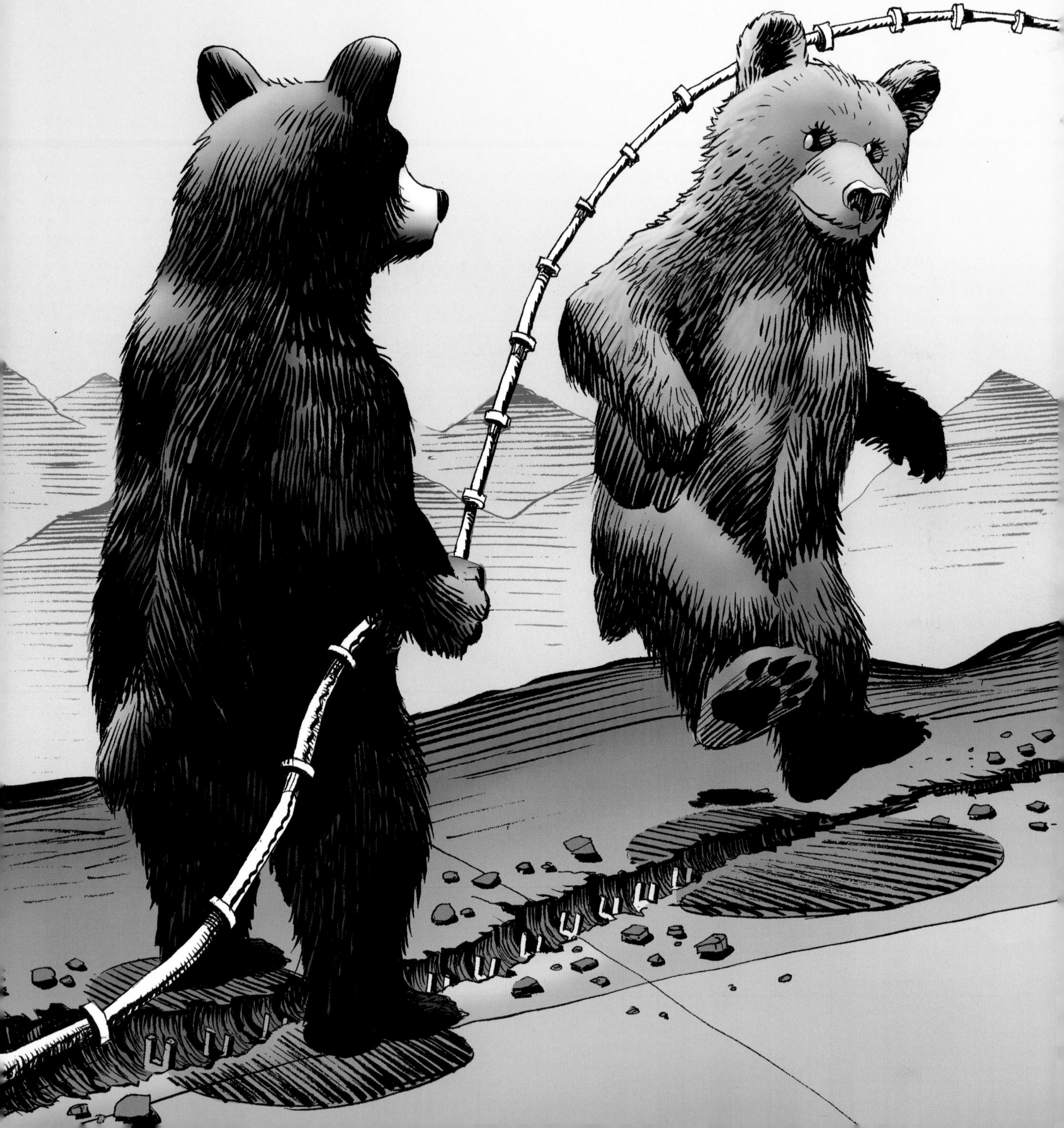

Jump-rope is a super fun game.
No oil will pass this way again.

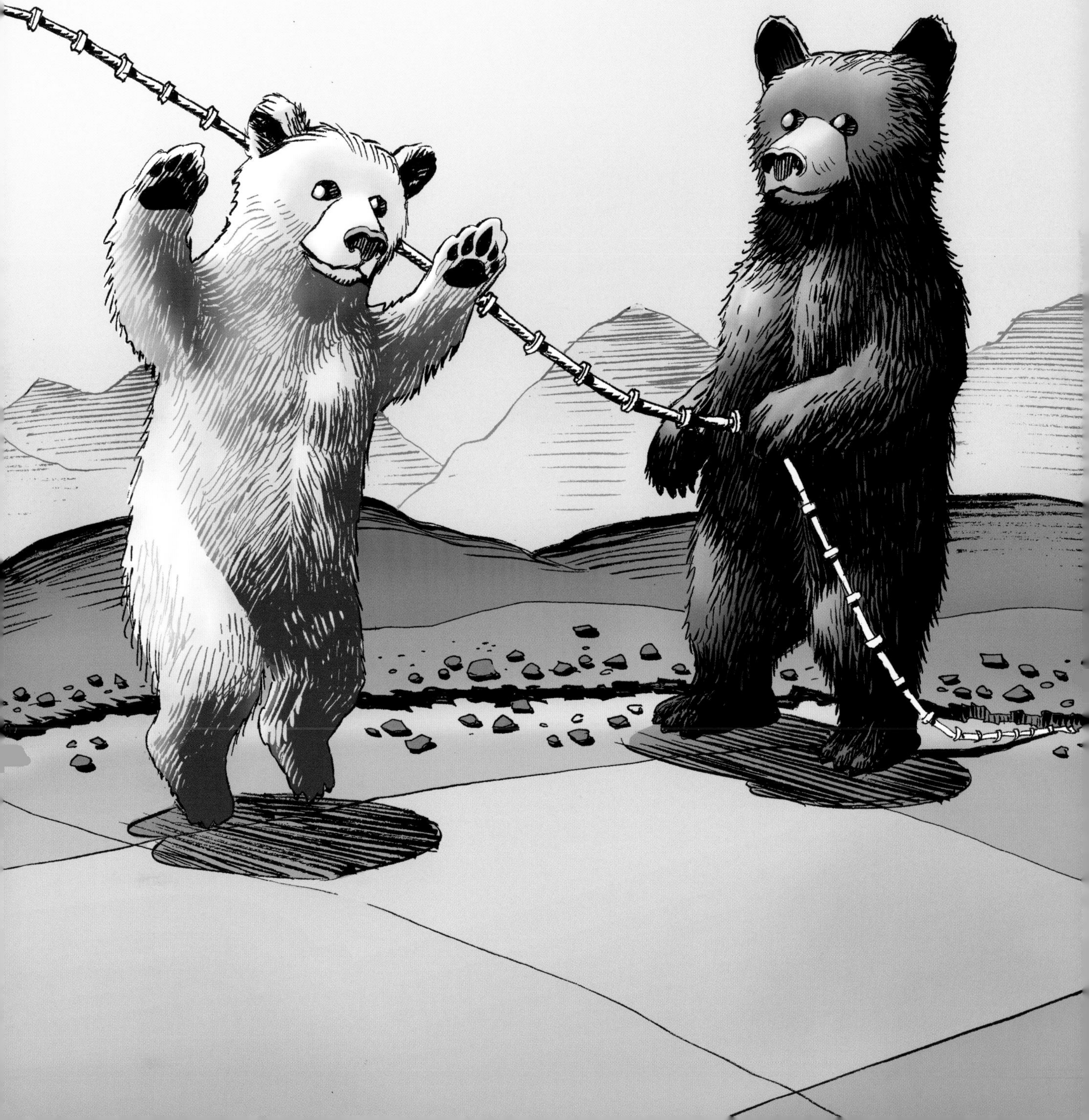

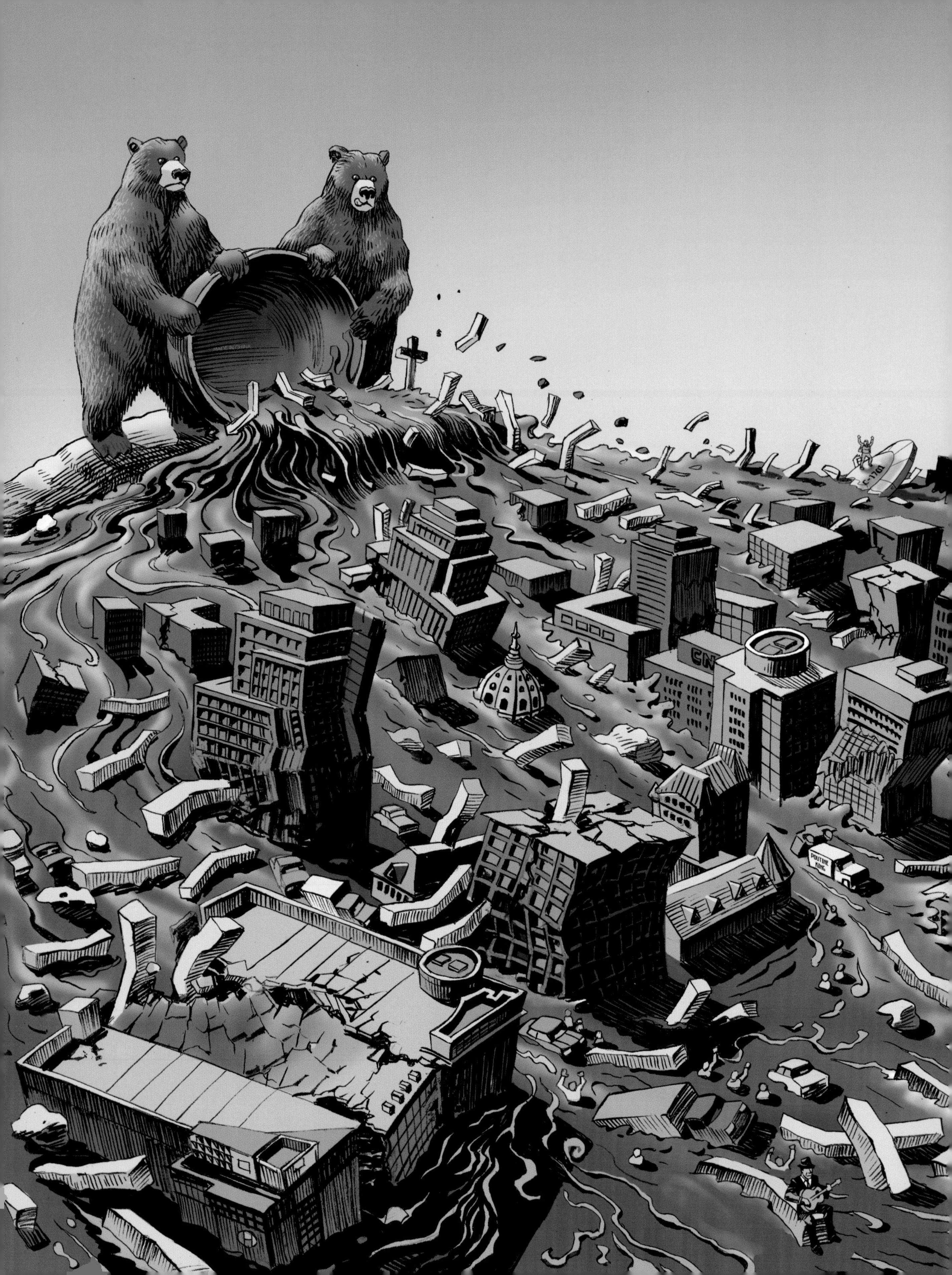
MADE IN CHINA
CN
C-1701
POUTINE KING

In Montreal, a foodie win!
As two bears drop their fresh poutine.

Fries, curds, gravy. Now we know.
A really delicious way to go.

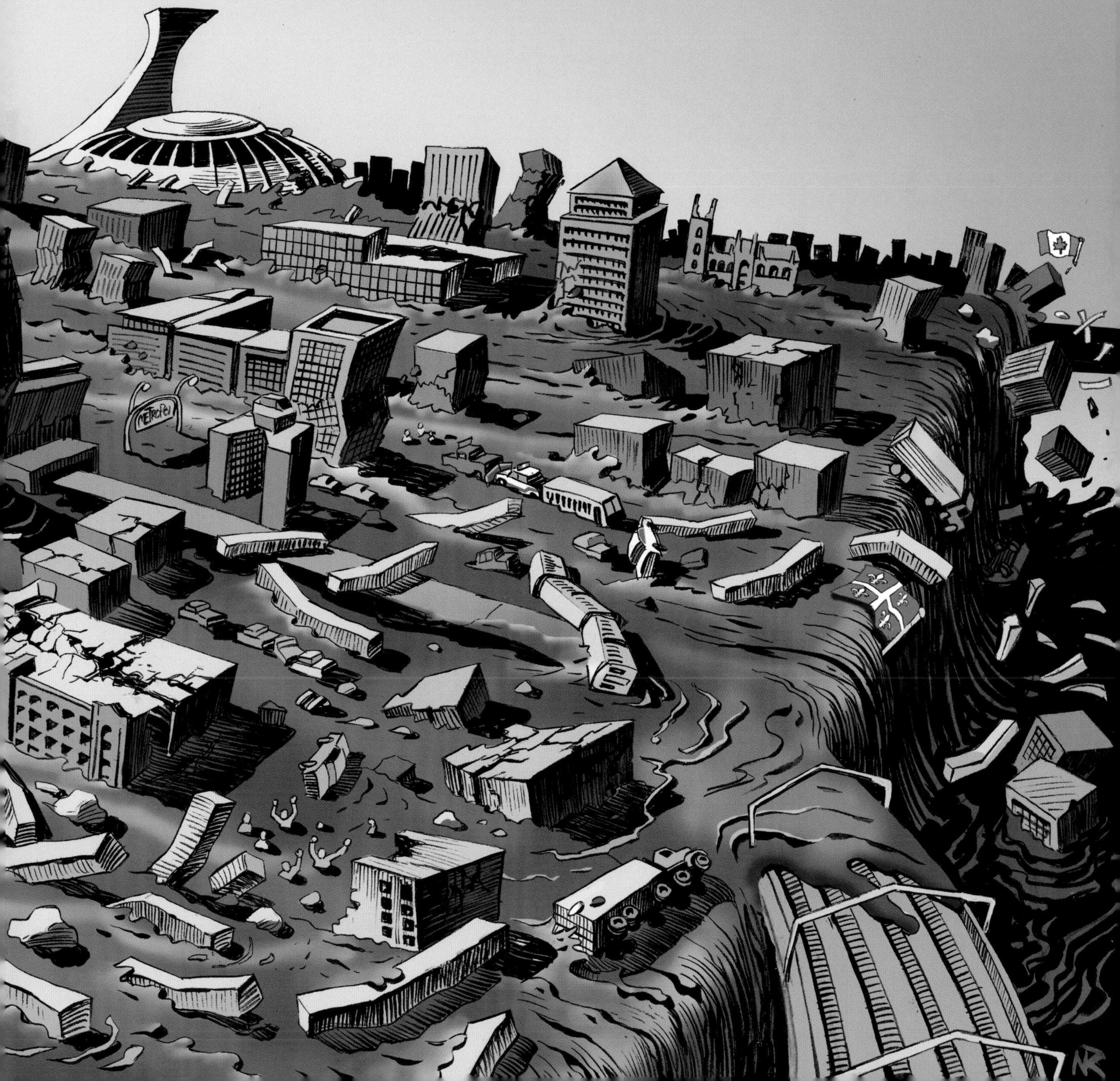

Our cities truly stomped to dust,
To sate the Bears vehement disgust.

Ottawa was saved till last.
The politicians were swallowed fast.

Plucked like ants from their nest.
Even the PM she did ingest.

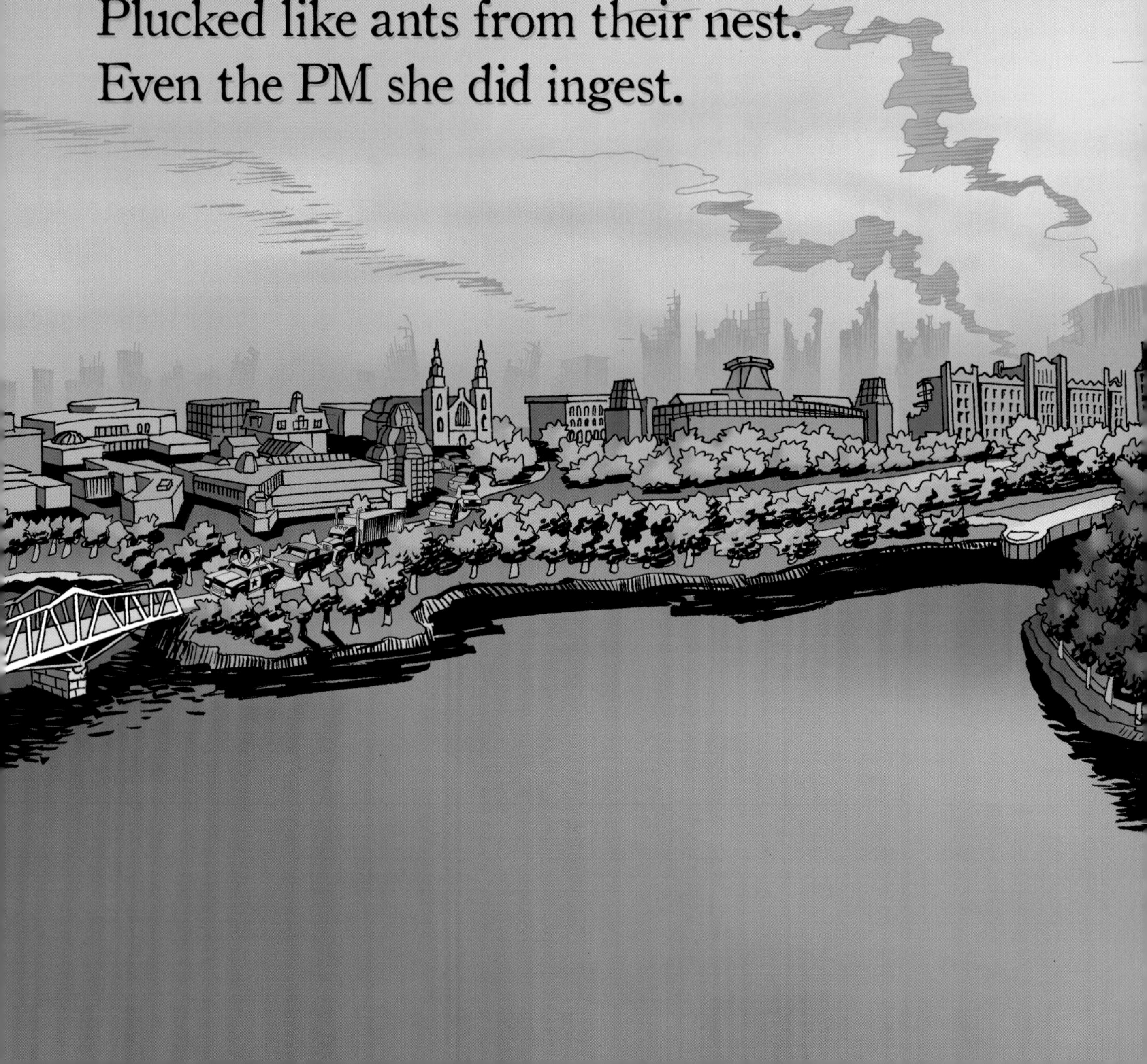

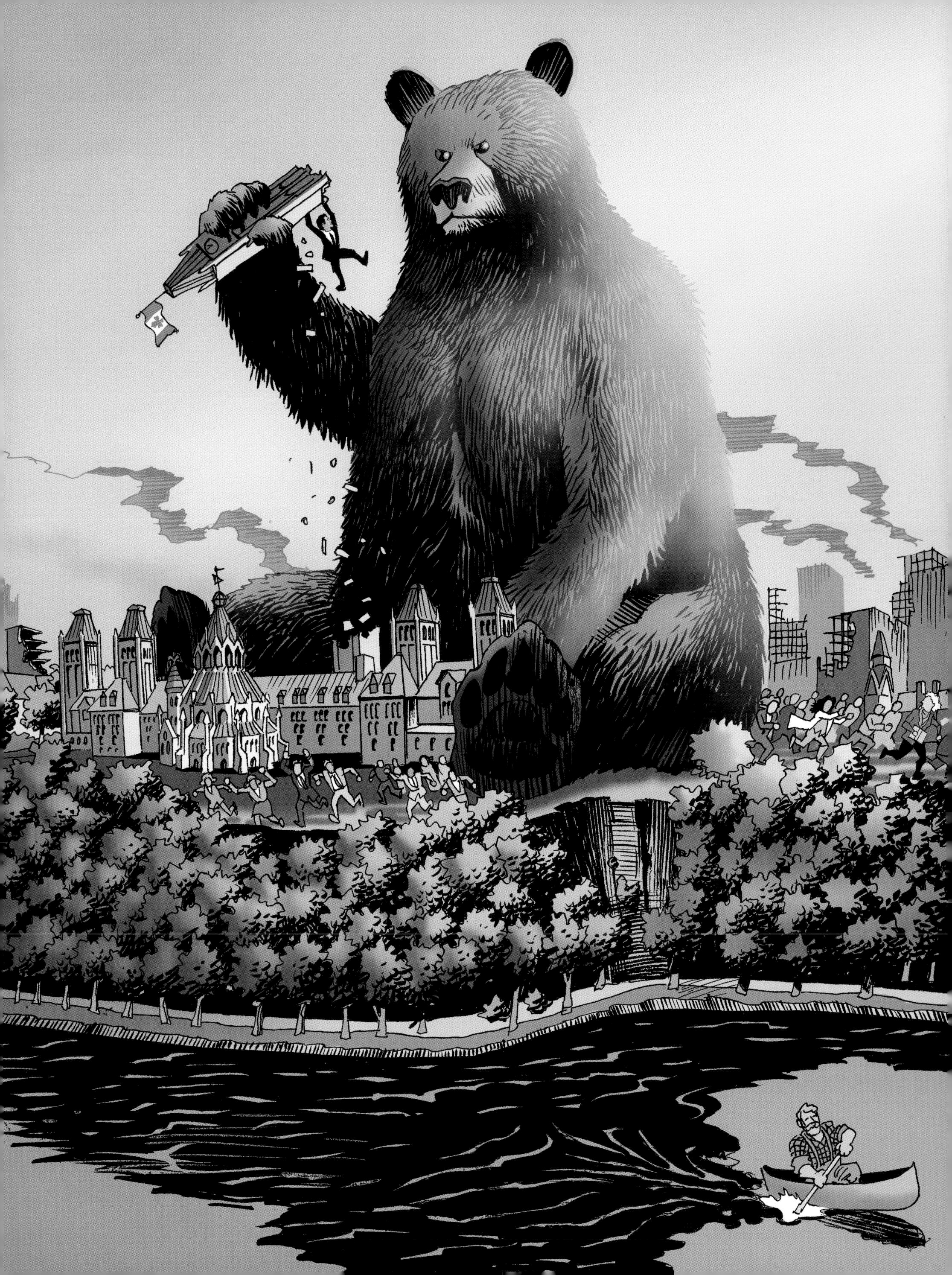

I tell you now with no hint of mirth.
The Rocky Mountains were ripped
from the earth.

Thrown down to the south, a wall of rock.
Gave the Americans quite a shock.

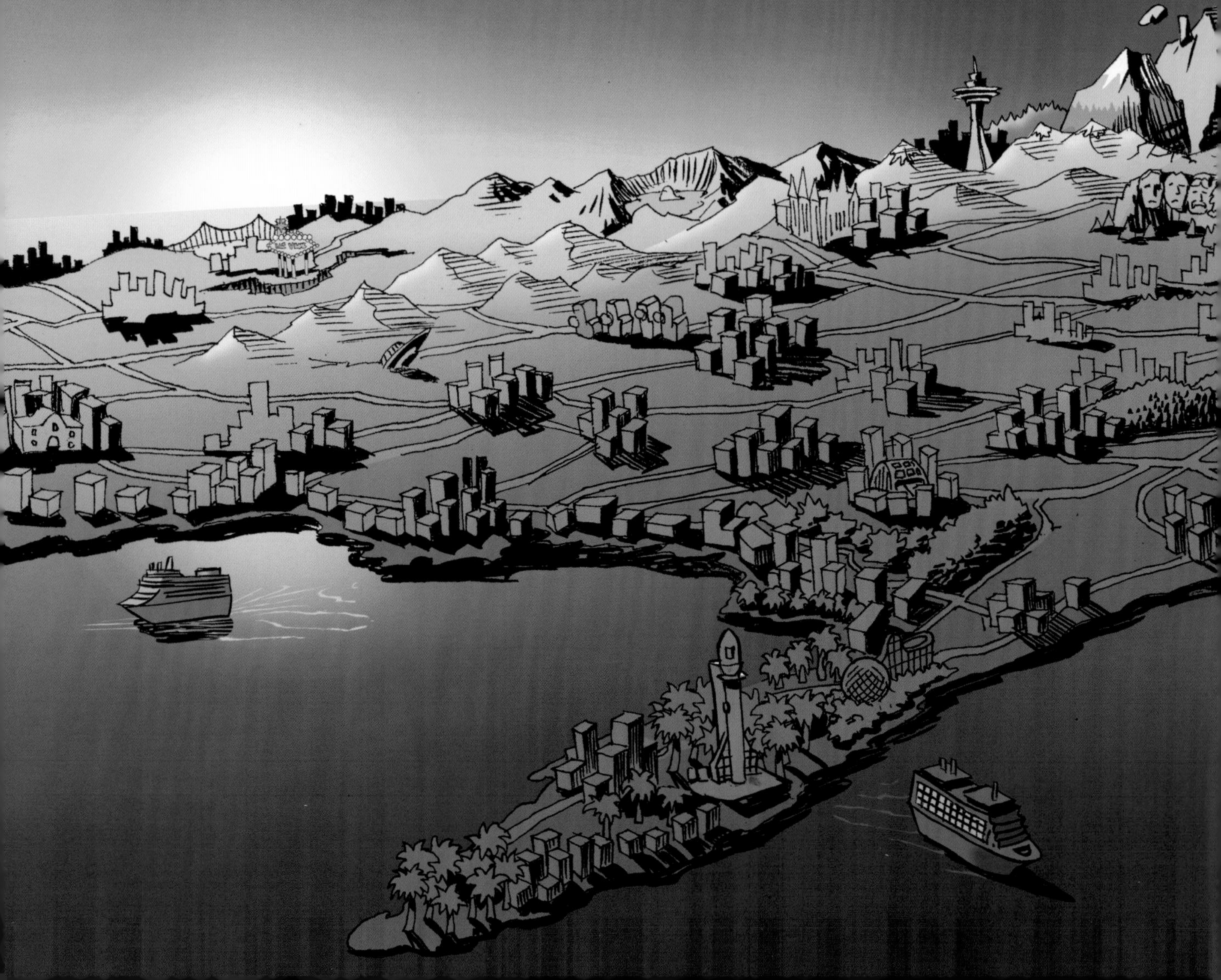

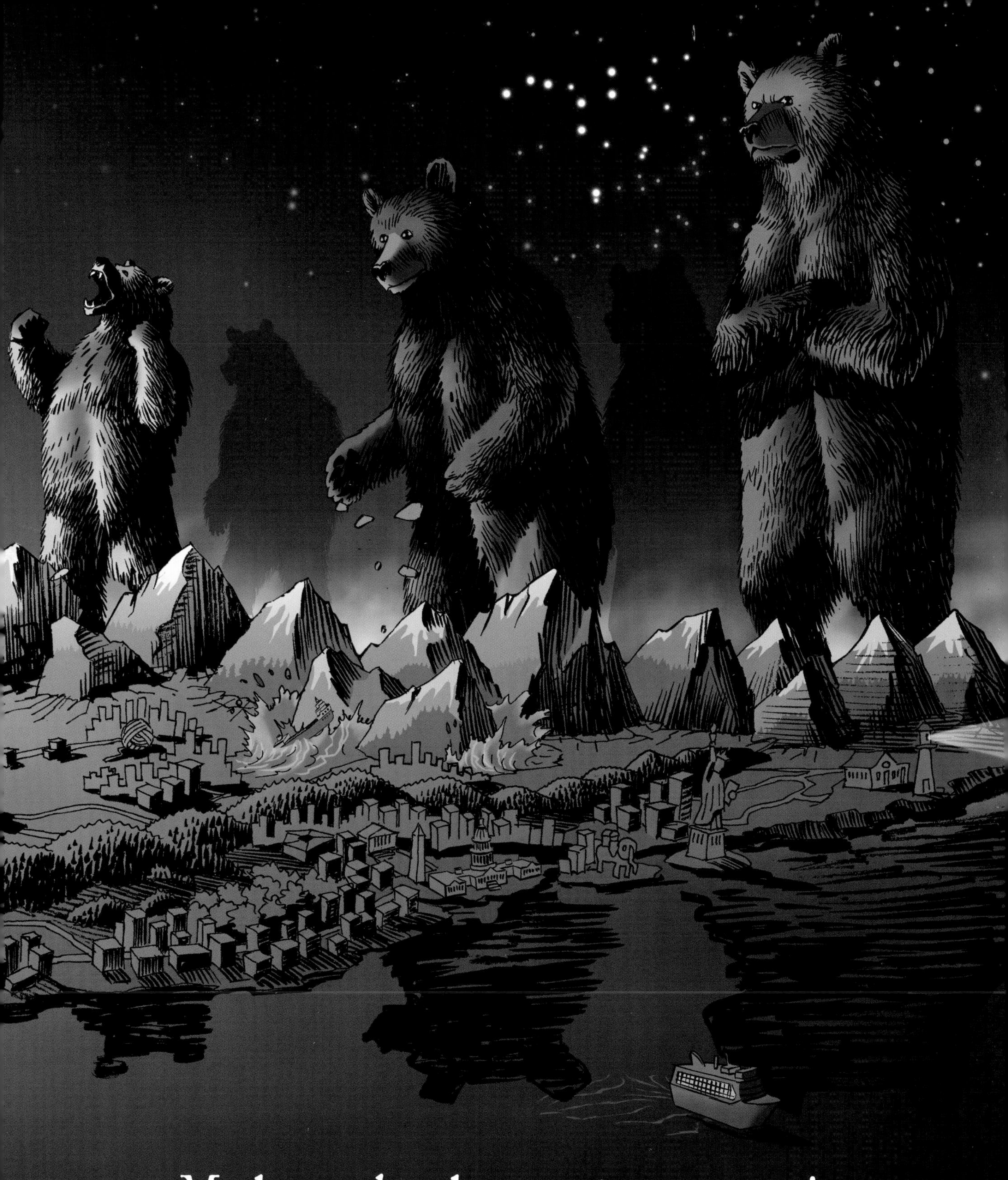

Made our border great once more!
And stifled our neighbours call for war.

That is how our story ends.
Please share this tale with your friends.

Lest they forget the lesson learned.
And Canada once more is burned.

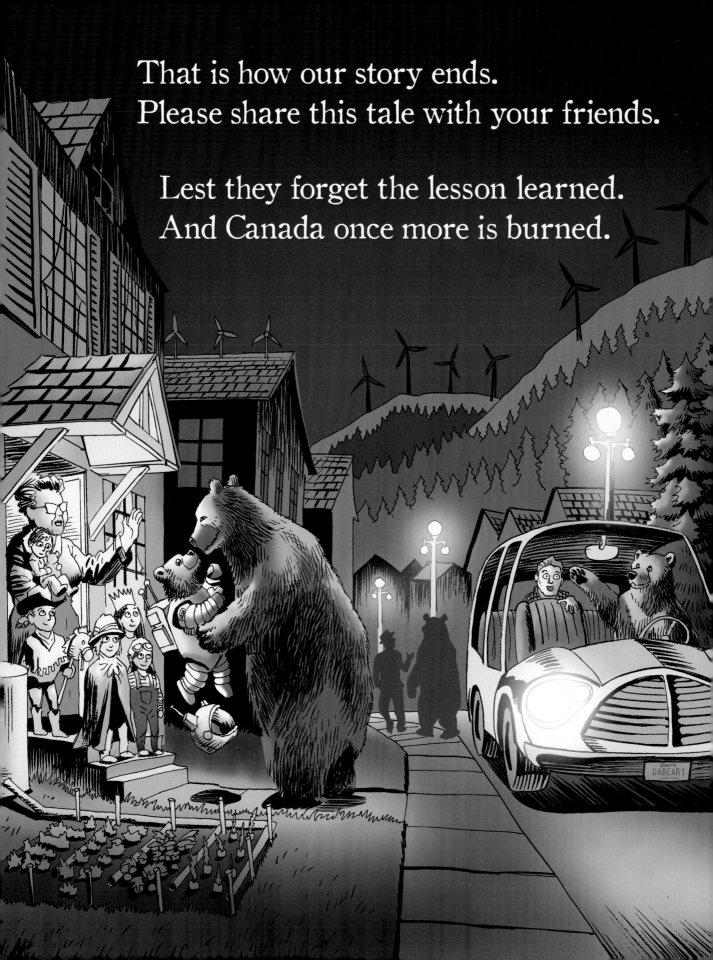